COMPUTER SCIENCE, TECHNOLOGY AND APPLICATIONS

DATA COLLECTION AND STORAGE

COMPUTER SCIENCE, TECHNOLOGY AND APPLICATIONS

Additional books in this series can be found on Nova's website under the Series tab.

Additional E-books in this series can be found on Nova's website under the E-books tab.

COMPUTER SCIENCE, TECHNOLOGY AND APPLICATIONS

DATA COLLECTION AND STORAGE

JULIAN R. EIRAS
EDITOR

Nova Science Publishers, Inc.
New York

Copyright © 2012 by Nova Science Publishers, Inc.

All rights reserved. No part of this book may be reproduced, stored in a retrieval system or transmitted in any form or by any means: electronic, electrostatic, magnetic, tape, mechanical photocopying, recording or otherwise without the written permission of the Publisher.

For permission to use material from this book please contact us:
Telephone 631-231-7269; Fax 631-231-8175
Web Site: http://www.novapublishers.com

NOTICE TO THE READER

The Publisher has taken reasonable care in the preparation of this book, but makes no expressed or implied warranty of any kind and assumes no responsibility for any errors or omissions. No liability is assumed for incidental or consequential damages in connection with or arising out of information contained in this book. The Publisher shall not be liable for any special, consequential, or exemplary damages resulting, in whole or in part, from the readers' use of, or reliance upon, this material. Any parts of this book based on government reports are so indicated and copyright is claimed for those parts to the extent applicable to compilations of such works.

Independent verification should be sought for any data, advice or recommendations contained in this book. In addition, no responsibility is assumed by the publisher for any injury and/or damage to persons or property arising from any methods, products, instructions, ideas or otherwise contained in this publication.

This publication is designed to provide accurate and authoritative information with regard to the subject matter covered herein. It is sold with the clear understanding that the Publisher is not engaged in rendering legal or any other professional services. If legal or any other expert assistance is required, the services of a competent person should be sought. FROM A DECLARATION OF PARTICIPANTS JOINTLY ADOPTED BY A COMMITTEE OF THE AMERICAN BAR ASSOCIATION AND A COMMITTEE OF PUBLISHERS.

Additional color graphics may be available in the e-book version of this book.

Library of Congress Cataloging-in-Publication Data

Data collection and storage / editor, Julian R. Eiras.
    p. cm.
Includes bibliographical references and index.
ISBN 978-1-61209-689-6 (softcover)
1. Databases. 2. Computer storage devices. 3. Science--Data processing.
I. Eiras, Julian R.
QA76.9.D32D3626 2011
004.5--dc23
                    2011032657

Published by Nova Science Publishers, Inc. † New York

CONTENTS

Preface		vii
Chapter 1	The Usefulness of Collecting Data From Discharge Abstracts to Estimate Cancer Incidence *Catherine Quantin, Eric Benzenine, Rachid Abbas, Béatrice Trombert, Mathieu Hagi, Bertrand Auverlot, Anne Marie Bouvier, Marcel Goldberg, and Jean Marie Rodrigues*	1
Chapter 2	Multiplexing Holograms for Data Page Storage *Elena Fernandez Varó, Manuel Pérez Molina, Rosa Fuentes Rosillo, Celia García Llopis, Augusto Beléndez Vázquez, and Inmaculada Pascual Villalobos*	27
Chapter 3	Novel Metallic Nanocluster-Based Structures and Semiconductor Thin Films for Information Storage *H. Khlyap, V. Laptev and L. Panchenko*	53
Chapter 4	The Influence of Bias Against Target Culture on Motivation of Young Learners to Learn English: Some Thoughts on Data Collection *Eda Üstünel and Seyran Öztürk*	71
Chapter 5	Animal and Seasonal Effectors of Cow Behavior in Dairy Houses: An Observational Collection *A. Nikkhah and R. Kowsar*	85

| **Chapter 6** | Swift Collection and Quantification of Cow Cervix Morphology Data: Validating a Practical Apparatus
A. Nikkhah and S. M. Karimzadeh | **95** |

Index **105**

PREFACE

This new book discusses data collection and storage across a broad spectrum of applications. Topics discussed include the collection of mortality data in relation to cancer prevalence and incidence to achieve successful national health policies; a study of the basic elements needed for a holographic data storage system; metallic nanocluster-based structures and semiconductor thin films for information storage and swift collection and quantification of cow cervix morphology data.

Chapter 1- Every modern country needs reliable health information to allow effective health care management (regarding population and infrastructures), to improve public health policies (by gathering and evaluating data), to provide health professionals with an accurate view of their activity, and, more widely, to educate the population. These data are also essential for scientific research (*i.e.* epidemiology, drug monitoring, health economics and sociology, *etc.*), which, in turn, could give insights into policies and professionals' activity.

Chapter 2- We live in the age of information science and new technologies, in which the use of computers music players, video, and data storage memory for information processing and storage has become something quotidian. The users of these technologies store large amounts of digital data. In addition, huge amounts of data on the banks, companies, or government archives are stored on devices that occupy a large space, which could be reduced if the devices had a higher storage capacity per unit volume. Conventional optical memory technologies like CD-ROMs and DVDs are two-dimensional surface-storage techniques, and thus they have almost reached the limit of their capacity and become obsolete. This fact has encouraged world researchers to focus on new techniques to design devices with larger storage capacity, as it is the case of holographic storage devices. These devices can store the entire volume of the informational material thereby increasing the storage capacity in comparison with two-dimensional devices that only store the information on the surface. Companies such as Bayer and InPhase came together to create the Tapestry^{TM} [1,2], the first prototype of a holographic optical storage system that is being used by leading companies and is capable of storing 200 Gbytes to 1.6 Tbytes in a disk 130 mm of diameter.

Chapter 3- How to store information? This age-old question existed since human beings first started to make rock pictures. Now the problems of information storage are solved by novel nanophysics and nanotechnology. Among them high-temperature superconductivity and processes in metallic cluster-based nanostructures (for example, dark currents in metals under room temperature without external electric field [1]) open ways for principally new methods of information storage. One can select the following directions in the field: quantum computing, development of nanotube-based memory devises, and pulse holography. Thw authors briefly sketch these directions and then present unique experimental results, which can provide a good base for designing perspective memory and information storage devices.

Chapter 4- For years many theories have been put forward to explain how people acquire their first language. It has been accepted that there is a critical age period in first language acquisition which is ideal time for acquiring the language properly. But for second language acquisition, it is still debatable whether there is such a period in second language acquisition or not. However, it is generally accepted that the earlier the better. With the developments in the political, economical, technological areas, today world is getting shrinking, so people need to be in contact with other countries and to do this they need a medium language which is mostly accepted today, English. For these reasons, with the educational reform in Turkey in 1997-1998 education year, teaching English in Turkey was agreed to be started at the 4th grade.

Chapter 5- In mechanized modern dairy facilities with competitive environments, monitoring behavior is an opportunity to manipulate and optimize nutritional, health and social status of high-merit cows. Initiative older research on cattle social behavior (Schmisseur et al., 1966; Arave and Albright, 1976; Arave et al., 1974; Lamb, 1976; Arave and Albright, 1981; Pennigton and Albright, 1985), although very insufficient, highlighted and in some aspects quantified associations of cow physiology, social rank, immunity and performance with cow surroundings, including stalls design and space, inter-group member changes, isolation, and other stressors. The newer research shed light on how cow-grouping strategies affect social and feeding behaviors (Phillips and Rind, 2001; Albright, 1993; Grant and Albright. 2001). Most recently, renewed research interests on cow feed intake and social behavior have promised improvements in health, metabolism and production (Endres and Barberg, 2007; Huzzey et al., 2007; von Keyserlingk et al., 2008; Goldhawk et al., 2009). For instance, Huzzey et al. (2007) showed that DMI and eating activity as well as engagement in social and aggressive interactions at feed bunk during the precalving week decrease in cows that are at high risk of mastitis postpartum. Similarly, Goldhawk et al. (2009) found that cows with 1) reduced DMI, 2) decreased frequency of feed bunk visits and 3) shorter feed bunk visits during the precalving week exhibited subclinical ketosis for few weeks around parturition. These studies suggest that social and feeding behaviors may affect and be affected by cow health and productivity. Thus, such behaviors can effectively be monitored as a management tool to evaluate and improve cow health and longevity, especially in large herds. Data are lacking on how environmental factors independently or in relation to cow factors (e.g., production level, parity, lactation stage) affect social-feeding behaviors. The authors hypothesized that lactating cows housed in large groups exhibit different eating, ruminating, and resting or social activities during different seasons. In addition, the authors hypothesized that such activities will depend on lactation stage, milk production level, and cow parity. Therefore, an observational study was conducted from December 2006 to February 2008 with the objective to collect and determine seasonal eating, ruminating, resting, standing and idle activities in lactating cows of different physiological stages.

Chapter 6-. The progressive advancements in the ruminant science and industry necessitate innovative, accurate and rapid technologies that can improve reproduction management. Simultaneous achievement of efficient production and reproduction has been a major challenge to dairy farmers (Moore and Thatcher, 2006; Studer, 1998). For instance, for many of today's dairy farmers, a favorable calving interval is about 12-13 months (Norman et al., 2009; Strandberg and Oltenacu, 1989), which may not necessarily be optimum under given circumstances. To achieve such an interval, cows should not be under much stressful physiological and environmental conditions, such as heat and metabolic stresses (Jordan, 2003; Moore and Thatcher, 2006).

In: Data Collection and Storage
Editor: Julian R. Eiras

ISBN 978-1-61209-689-6
© 2012 Nova Science Publishers, Inc.

Chapter 1

THE USEFULNESS OF COLLECTING DATA FROM DISCHARGE ABSTRACTS TO ESTIMATE CANCER INCIDENCE

Catherine Quantin[a, b], Eric Benzenine[b], Rachid Abbas[b], Béatrice Trombert[c], Mathieu Hagi[b], Bertrand Auverlot[b], Anne Marie Bouvier[d, e], Marcel Goldberg[f], and Jean Marie Rodrigues[c]*

[a] Inserm, U866, Dijon, F-21000, Univ de Bourgogne, Dijon, F-21000, France, 03.80.29.34.65, 03.80.29.39.73
[b] CHRU, Service de Biostatistique et d'Informatique Médicale, Dijon, France, 03.80.29.34.65, 03.80.29.39.73
[c] Biostatistique, Information Médicale et Technologies de la Communication, Université Jean Monnet, St Etienne, France
[d] CHU (University Hospital), F-21079 Dijon, France ;
[e] INSERM U866, Registre des cancers digestifs, Dijon, BP 87900 F-21079, France
[f] Inserm U1018, Epidemiology of occupational and social determinants of health - Centre for Research in Epidemiology and Population Health, 16 avenue Paul Vaillant Couturier, F-94807, Villejuif, France, Versailles-Saint Quentin University, Versailles, France

---

[*] Email: catherine.quantin@chu-dijon.fr

ABSTRACT

Accurate, precise and timely information related to cancer prevalence and incidence is the most important key to achieving successful national health policies. Mortality data, available at the national level in most countries around the world, are the main source of information. However, statistical information on mortality is limited for many reasons, and it must be used with caution in cancer epidemiology. For example, it is difficult to identify the underlying or contributing cause of death for a patient with cancer, and particularly for elderly patients with multiple pathologies. Moreover, the diagnosed cancer is not mentioned in death certificates if the death is due to another cause. Mortality data are poor indicators of the incidence of cancers that have a good prognosis.

Thanks to morbidity data in registries, which are regularly published in "Cancer Incidence in Five Continents", cancers are thought to be well described worldwide. In many countries, because registries only partially cover the concerned population, epidemiologists have looked for additional sources of information. Administrative data, recorded in standardized coded databases at the regional or national level, are available in most industrialised countries. The fact that these data are used for budget allocation to hospitals encourages improved data quality in terms of coherence, precision and exhaustiveness.

The purpose of the first section of this treatise is to describe the currently available administrative data around the world: which country collects what data? What is the initial aim of the data selection? What populations are concerned?

The second section focuses on epidemiological use of these data and more particularly, the estimation of cancer incidence: What algorithms are used to estimate the incidence thanks to DRG data? What patterns can be used to estimate cancer incidence at the national level?

The interest of administrative data is now well understood by epidemiologists. This paper shows the usefulness of DRG databases and underlines the interest and difficulties of using these data to estimate cancer incidence. In particular, the utilisation of these data requires awareness of how - and why -they are collected, to better appraise the potential biases and the overall data quality. Moreover, administrative databases cannot be used as a unique source to assess cancer incidence. The use of other sources, such as cancer registries, is fundamental both to validate algorithms based on DRG data and to develop models.

1. INTRODUCTION

Every modern country needs reliable health information to allow effective health care management (regarding population and infrastructures), to improve public health policies (by gathering and evaluating data), to provide health professionals with an accurate view of their activity, and, more widely, to educate the population. These data are also essential for scientific research (*i.e.* epidemiology, drug monitoring, health economics and sociology, *etc.*), which, in turn, could give insights into policies and professionals' activity.

Data could be provided by surveys, but as these are planned (even in the long term) they do not match the timeless approach inherent in benchmark-based improvement. Besides being limited in time, surveys are undertaken for some specific purpose, which means specific outcomes that may be unsuitable for other miscellaneous concerns.

Using data generated during the day-to-day activities of the whole health care system could be a different but useful approach, as the data are already collected for financial purpose. Thus, the statistical information is not only structured to meet the needs of deciders, but also results from the country's existing administrative procedures.

In order to explain the current statistical information system, we will begin our presentation by describing the main features of the organization and its evolution.

Section 1 focuses on exhaustive health databases and essentially include administrative sources of data: morbidity data collected from management files, particularly from hospitals. The objective of this first section is to describe existing administrative data gathered around the world (*e.g.* the Diagnosis-Related Groups: DRGs) and to clarify some points: which country collects what data? What is the initial objective of data collection? What populations are concerned?

The second section focuses on utilisation of the data for epidemiological purposes and more particularly on estimations of cancer incidence based on these data: what values are put into the algorithms used to estimate the incidence thanks to DRG data? What patterns could improve the quality of these algorithms and estimate cancer incidence at the national level?

2. COLLECTION OF ADMINISTRATIVE DATA IN DIFFERENT COUNTRIES

Administrative databases are used to record summarized information on characteristics of inpatient and outpatient hospitalization events (*e.g.* visits to or by physicians or independent health professionals, prescriptions filled, home care visits, nursing home stays).

2.1. Case Mix Databases

The system, known as the Diagnosis-Related Groups (DRG) or case mix system was developed at the end of the sixties by a team of researchers at Yale University under the direction of Robert Fetter and John Thompson with the aim of describing the hospital's products. The case mix system is a set of three tools:

- Minimum basic data set collection (e.g. case mix data base)
- Patient Classification System (e.g. DRG)
- Relative scale of average cost (e.g. Maryland cost weights)

In 1983, the DRG system was adopted to pay US hospitals for care provided. For the first time, one payer of the multipayer US health insurance system (Medicare, the social insurance program administered by the United States government, providing health insurance coverage to people who are aged 65 and over), had a way to compare the output of one hospital with that of another. When Congress adopted the DRG system, other countries took notice and soon a number of them began to experiment with various case mix systems directly or indirectly modeled on the DRG system. Nevertheless the use of this information system to pay hospitals came after one or two decades of use for other goals such as internal management, health care planning and epidemiologic and economic studies.

2.2. Which Country Collects What Data?

After the US, France, the UK, Portugal and Belgium were among the first to experiment the use of DRG in their own health systems. Today, a number of other countries, Germany among the most recent, have begun to use case mix systems, (Table 1).

Table 1. Case mix system characteristics according to country

Country	Year of start	Diagnosis coding	Procedure coding
United States	1967	ICD-9-CM	ICD-9-CM
France	1982	ICD-10	CCAM
Canada	1983	ICD-10-CA	CCI
Portugal	1984	ICD-9-CM	ICD-9-CM
Sweden	1985	ICD-10	NCSP
Australia	1986	ICD-10-AM	ICD-10-AM
United Kingdom	1987	ICD-10	OPCS 4
Belgium	1990	ICD-9-CM	ICD-9-CM
Hungary	1993	ICD-9	ICPM
New-Zealand	1993	ICD-10-AM	ICD-10-AM
Denmark	1994	ICD-10	NCSP
Italy	1994	ICD-9-CM	ICD-9-CM
Norway	1997	ICD-10	NCSP
Switzerland	1997	ICD-10	CHOP
Singapore	1997	ICD-9-CM	ICD-9-CM
Japan	2001	ICD-10	JPC
Germany	2005	ICD-10	ICPM

ICD-9-CM: International Classification of Disease 9th revision clinical modification
ICD-10: International Classification of Disease 10th revision
CCI: Canadian Classification of Health Intervention
CCAM: Common Classification of surgical procedures
ICNP: Nordic Classification of Surgical Procedures
ICD-10-AM: International Classification of Disease 10th revision Australian modification
OPCS: UK Classification of Interventions and Procedures
ICPM: International Classification of Procedures in Medicine
JPC: Japanese classification of procedures
CHOP Swiss Classification for Hospital Procedures

In all these countries, the first step was to set up the collection of descriptive variables in the form of a standardized discharge summary or uniform hospital discharge dataset. Every record of the case mix database includes:

- • Demographics (age, gender)
- • Admission and discharge (dates, arrival from, discharge to, deaths)
- • Special care (days, type of unit)
- • Diagnosis codes (main diagnosis and co-morbidities)
- • Intervention codes

Each country has its own coding rules to code pathologies and interventions using various classifications (Table 1).

2.3. The Initial Objective of Data Collection?

The main objective of case mix data, using various methods according to the country, is to finance healthcare: allocation of public hospital budgets (e.g. Portugal) or prospective payment (e.g. USA) where funding follows the patient.

Benchmarking is also a current objective to improve hospital cost-effectiveness (financial, length of stay comparisons) (e.g. Australia)

Internal management is increasingly based on case mix data for: analysis of hospital productivity (e.g. Denmark), improving hospital efficiency and effectiveness (e.g. Singapore), reducing the length of stay (e.g. Belgium), controlling growth of hospital costs and forecast hospital costs (e.g. Italy).

More rarely, it is a source of information for consumers to increase transparency, enable consumer-choice across the country (e.g. Sweden) and focus on quality of care (e.g. UK).

2.4. The Populations Concerned

While case mix data is collected in many countries for acute care, inpatient hospital care and day surgery, the use for payment can be restricted to some specifically insured populations (federal insurances Medicare for the over 65s and Medicaid for the poor but also certain Health Maintenance Organizations).

Case mix systems are continually being developed and improved in the areas of rehabilitation (USA, Canada, France), psychiatry (Sweden, Canada, Australia), outpatient care (USA, UK, Australia), emergency care (USA, UK, Australia, Hungary), ambulatory care (Canada), home care (USA, France), long-term care (USA, Hungary).

The generalization of the case mix system is sometimes limited to public hospitals (Portugal, Singapore). Variations according to the region (e.g. Sweden) is also observed, or according to the type of health insurance (USA) [1-3].

3. THE INTEREST OF ADMINISTRATIVE DATA FOR EPIDEMIOLOGY: APPLICATIONS FOR THE ESTIMATION OF CANCER INCIDENCE

In many developed countries population registries can provide information on the incidence of cancers and its variations over time [4-6] . When these data are not available, or are available only in restricted areas, mortality data are used.

3.1. Advantages and Limits of Data Classically Used in Epidemiology

3.1.1. Cancer Registries

In most cases, cancer registries are managed in accordance with the recommendations of the International Agency for Research on Cancer (IARC), and in Europe, according to the recommendations of the European Network of Cancer Registries. Registries include all cases of new invasive tumours diagnosed in patients residing in the geographical area they cover. The main data sources are the databases of public and private pathology and cytology laboratories, hospitals and clinics and those of the National Health Insurance Service, when possible. To ensure the quality of data, doubloons, coherence, and missing data checks are regularly done.

These data are regularly used to update national and international statistics [7]. However, except for countries where national registries have been set up such as the Netherlands, Sweden, the Czech Republic and Ireland, registries cover only a small proportion of the whole population. and /or restricted areas *i.e.* not all regions are covered. Thus, it is difficult to extrapolate the incidence measured in registries to the national level. Only district-limited estimates of the incidence of cancers are then based on morbidity data from cancer registries, and only for districts covered by a registry.

The national estimates of cancer incidence are thus often based on mortality data, when these data are exhaustively collected [8].

3.1.2. Mortality Data

Mortality is the most commonly used indicator to describe the health of a population. Mortality data are provided annually worldwide and yield descriptions of the death characteristics, death trends and geographical distributions of causes. Such data can also be used to compare mortality rates of different countries. This is facilitated by the homogeneous methods of data collection using international death certificates, for example, which use the same classifications to code the causes of death. The data production process starts with the medical certification of causes of death provided by physicians. This is the basic information. Causes of death are then coded by nosology specialists and made available to researchers and other health specialists.

Statistical information on mortality is limited for many reasons [9], and it must be used with caution in cancer epidemiology. For example, it is difficult to identify the underlying or contributing cause of death for a patient with cancer, and particularly for elderly patients with multiple pathologies. Moreover, the diagnosed cancer is not mentioned in death certificates if the cause of death is due to another disease or an accident [10]. Mortality data are also poor indicators of the incidence of cancers that have a good prognosis.

At the regional level, many difficulties can be encountered when national mortality data are used to estimate cancer incidence. Changes in diagnostic and therapeutic procedures from one district to another can affect the calculation of both cancer incidence and the incidence/mortality ratio. This particularly concerns screened cancers, because of improved patient care thanks to systematic screening programs. As screening was implemented at different periods and in different ways in each district, the incidence/ mortality ratio is a poor indicator to estimate cancer incidence in each district. Another indicator should then be envisaged so as to study geographical variations in cancer incidence.

3.2. Advantages and Limits of DRG Data to Estimate Cancer Incidence

3.2.1. Potential Advantages

Some authors have proposed using discharge abstracts gathered in hospitals through the DRG Systems to estimate cancer incidence [11-18]. Even though they do not contain key data such as socio-economic status, DRG databases have a major interest in terms of public health [9] for various purposes, including research.

DRG systems often provide standardized coded and structured databases at the national level. The fact that these data are used for budget allocation to hospitals encourages improved data quality in terms of coherence, precision and exhaustiveness. Thus these data are often close to 100% exhaustive with regard to the total number of hospitalisations in each hospital. Regarding quality assessment based on the literature, the gross error rate related to collecting and coding diagnoses and procedures is decreasing over time [20-34]. In addition to quality assurance programmes in some health structures [35,36], subsequent quality control procedures on samples, often carried out within hospitals or externally make it possible to detect most errors that have a financial impact. Patients diagnosed with cancer are well represented through DRG data, as they are often hospitalised.

3.2.2. Limits of Using DRG Data to Estimate Cancer Incidence

The use of discharge abstracts gathered in hospitals to calculate cancer incidence, particularly in districts without population registries, has already been addressed [8, 11-14, 28-32, 37-39], but no clear conclusions were drawn.

The potential interest of DRG databases appears clearly since they provide coded, structured and standardized personal medical data, but important methodological considerations and data validation work are required. Thus, several conditions should be guaranteed. Leaving aside legal problems associated with access to personal data, and technical difficulties of matching data from different sources, which we shall comment upon in section 4, the issue of quality and validity of the health data deserves attention.

Data originally collected for administrative purposes are usually accurately validated for financial reasons. In contrast, the quality of the medical information is not necessarily checked closely enough for epidemiological purposes. Despite the fact that these databases have not been systematically validated, a few specific epidemiological studies have been carried out on data from DRG databases. Using DRG data as a source for pathologies is complex as the diagnosis is not always reliable. For example, if DRG data are used to estimate the incidence (new cases) of a given pathology, prevalent cases must be excluded by searching through earlier DRG data.

Most of the limits of using DRG data for the selection of incident cancer cases that were underlined by preceding studies are not specific to cancer. These difficulties can also be encountered when other diseases treated in hospitals are studied [21, 22, 24, 33, 34, 40-44].

The first difficulty lies is the creation of algorithms that allow the detection of incident cancer cases, and for this purpose, different identification methods have been proposed in the literature. Some are based on a search through patients' hospitalisation DRGs for the first occurrence of a cancer diagnosis code [38, 45-47]. However, these approaches have to cope with errors in DRG data collection, related to the hierarchy of diagnoses or to coding errors (*e.g.* different codes stand for in-situ or secondary tumours....). To avoid errors related to diagnosis hierarchy (*e.g.* the distinction between principal and secondary diagnosis), some algorithms were designed to search for a diagnosis whatever its position in the discharge abstract, excluding prevalent cases thanks to linkage with previous hospitalizations[48, 49].

Other methods rely on complex algorithms that mix diagnosis and procedure codes [14, 37, 38, 47, 50-52]. Most of them detect cancer cases by the association between a diagnosis of cancer and a surgical procedure specific to this cancer. As a specific procedure cannot be defined for all cancers, another suggestion was to exclude [48], radiotherapy and chemotherapy from the algorithm to avoid overestimations of the number of incident cases.

The second difficulty of using DRG data to estimate cancer incidence is due to the time gap (sometimes very large) between the date of diagnosis recorded in the registry and the date of hospitalisation recorded in the DRG database. To be retrievable in the DRG, a cancer case has to be specified in a discharge abstract, *i.e.* has to be diagnosed during a hospitalisation. A patient could thus be included as a case by the registry but not recorded in the DRG data base if, for example, a diagnosis is made by a general practitioner in

December, and the patient is then hospitalised for this cancer in January. In such cases, the patient will be included in the registry for a specific year 'n', but will only be selected by our algorithms for the year 'n+1'. Therefore, to take into account this time gap, some algorithms [48] that considered consecutive years were tested. Such algorithms showed improved sensitivity and positive predictive values. Some patients who were misclassified as false positives during the analysis on one year became true positives, when consecutive data were merged, which explains the improvement in the positive predictive value. However, an exploratory analysis of false positives and negatives we made [48], showed that the number of false positives misclassified due to the time gap was counterbalanced by the number of false negatives also related to this time gap, so that the total estimated number of incident cases was close to the one acquired from the registry. The improvement regarding the estimation of the number of new cancer cases was not as great as expected.

The third difficulty is related to inter-regional or inter-district variations in incidence rates. When DRG are collected only in specific areas, extrapolation of the results to the whole population may be exposed to several biases. The French study conducted by Uhry [53] relating to estimated cancer incidence compared the total numbers of cases in districts' registries with those estimated from DRG data. It showed considerable variability from one district to another. Though some of these differences may have been due to patients being hospitalized outside their district of residence, no real explanation of the discordances between DRG and registry data could be given in this study because it was impossible to link registry and DRG data, and it was not possible to refer to medical files. In a another French study [48], we confirmed the considerable variability from one district to another (differences ranging from 5 to 10% in sensitivity and positive predictive values) and found that the main reason for the discordance was that registries only consider the patient's residence at the time of the diagnosis, whereas DRG data consider the place where the health care is provided. Thanks to linkage, they quantified patients hospitalised outside their district of residence and assessed the impact of these patients on the outcomes: only a few patients (less than 5%) were not selected because they were hospitalised in another district. Furthermore, these patients were hospitalized outside their district of residence mostly to benefit from the care provided in a high reputation centre. In fact, migration was very low in these French rural districts, especially for elderly breast cancer patients. Beyond this geographical aspect, inter-district variability may also be due to differences in coding practices, as suggested by Misset et al. [21] who found that coding of medical diagnoses varied from one observer to another. However, these differences in coding practices may essentially stem from the hierarchy of diagnoses and/or the precision of codes. These issues can be overcome using complex algorithms as seem before.

The fourth difficulty is related to time-related variations in cancer incidence and to the quality of DRG data. When our results [48] were compared with those previously published by Couris and et al. [13] related to the estimate of breast cancer incidence, we found a difference in sensitivity estimates of about 10% (initial value in 2002: 64%) between 2002 and 2004 when the same algorithm based on the principal diagnosis and therapeutic procedures was used. As the incidence of breast cancer in the studied districts is quite close, and the data quality very similar, it was concluded that the increase in sensitivity between these two years was mainly due to improvement in the quality of DRG data.This improvement in data quality essentially results from the increasing use of the DRG for financial purposes, in accordance with the government's health policy.

The fifth difficulty is to extrapolate data collected according to sociodemographic criteria to other types of populations. For example, in the US, administrative data are collected in specific subpopulations (cf section2) according to different criteria (such as age for Medicare or precariousness for Medicaid). Some authors found that the Medicare population over the age of 65 differs in several important ways from the US Census estimates of the elderly population as a whole. The fact that only 95 to 96 percent of US elderly residents are enrolled in Medicare has previously been reported, but by breaking down data by age, gender, or race, it has been shown that Medicare coverage varies substantially across these groups [54].

The sixth difficulty is to obtain complete data on patients who are not systematically hospitalized for their cancer. In some countries, some patients may not be identified by DRG data, because they have never been treated for their cancer (some elderly patients), or if they are diagnosed and treated outside hospitals. This problem concerns some cancer locations (*e.g.* non melanoma skin cancers), some age classes (*e.g.* seniors) or some districts (*e.g.* rural areas). For example, a 90–year-old person suffering from prostate cancer may not be hospitalized, especially so if he lives in a rural area. To address this issue and obtain more complete information, data collected from general practitioners may be useful. For example, The Health Improvement Network (THIN) in the UK has created a medical research database of anonymized patient records from general practices. THIN contains medical data on a total of more 6 million subjects, of whom more than 2.5 million are actively registered with the practices and can be prospectively followed. The THIN database is believed to be representative of the UK population, containing data on approximately 4% of the UK population. Since 2003, THIN has made data available for epidemiologic research, and studies show that, regarding the incidence of all cancers combined, records in the THIN database are consistent with those of cancer registries [55, 56]. Thus, in France, linkage between hospital administrative data and the network of the association of French General Practitioners is currently drawing attention.

To account for all these difficulties, the linkage of DRG and registry data could provide a validation of the estimation of cancer incidence obtained from DRG data, the gold standard being the registry.

This linkage requires that the same identifier be used in the two databases, which is not often the case. In all countries where the same national identification number is used for administrative data and registry data, this linkage is not an issue. It is often the case for countries where national registries have been set up and where a national identification number is used for a wide range of purposes besides health. For example, most northern European countries (Finland, Denmark, Luxembourg …) use the national identity number for health purposes. In Denmark [57], a personal identifier (CPR-number) is used in most databases to identify a Danish citizen for his whole life. In some countries, like the United Kingdom, a specific national patient identification number is used, while the Netherlands and Ireland are planning to create one. In southern European countries, patient identification is based on region-specific patient identifiers. This makes data linkage possible at the individual level.

In the USA, linkage between participating cancer registries of the Surveillance Epidemiology and End Results Program (SEER) and Medicare and Medicaid data has been ongoing for 15 years in the framework of the United States' SEER-Medicare database [58]. The input of DRG data would then complete registry data by providing exhaustive information on hospital care to provide screening information [59] and care information[60-66]. This linkage was achievable because of the availability of the same variables (social security number, first and second names, first and middle names, dates of birth and death) in both databases.

But in most other countries, this linkage between DRG and registry data is not so easy to set up . For example, in France, a few years ago the national health insurance organization set up a national information system that gathered together data on hospitalisations and ambulatory care. However, the identification variables used in this national information system are the social security number of the insured person, the date of birth and the gender of the patient, and as these variables cannot be recorded in French registry databases because of privacy law, it is not possible to directly link the national information system and registry databases. In a recent work [48] we had to go back to the original data in each hospital and collect patients' first and second names and dates of birth, in addition to DRG data. We also had to use specific software [67,68], based on hash coding techniques to render them anonymous inside hospitals before exportation. The same procedure was used in registries. The probabilistic linkage model developed initially by Jaro [67-69] was used to take into account identity entry errors. Hopefully, France, like Belgium, is developing a project to create national patient identifiers specifically for healthcare by rendering the social security number anonymous.

3.2.3. What Modeling Can Be Used to Estimate Cancer Incidence at the National Level

3.2.3.1. Incidence Correction Using the Sensitivity and Specificity of Administrative Data

This method requires the sensitivity and specificity of administrative data to be estimated. These estimations suppose that a gold standard, based on cancer registries, for example, can list all incident cancer cases of the studied population [70,71].

For example, a corrected number of incident cancer cases was proposed [72] using the following formula:

$$= \frac{K - (1 - Sp)N}{Se + Sp - 1}$$

where N is the number of inhabitants of the general population; K is the number of cases identified in the DRG-provided database with one of the algorithms among N. However, this number can be inaccurate, but thanks to a Bayesian approach, a corrected estimate and a credibility interval can be provided.

3.2.3.2. Identifying Factors of Incidence Variation by Adjusting for Factors of Variation through Statistical Modeling

However, as registries do not always cover the entire population, it was proposed to adjust for inter-district factors of variation through statistical modeling.

Before creating models, it is preferable to identify these factors and explore the reasons for any discordance [48] between DRG and registry data, so as to understand the limits of using DRG data to estimate cancer incidence. For this exploratory analysis of false negatives and false positives, observed from the linkage between DRG and registry data, it is necessary to go back to gathered medical files to determine the reasons for the inaccuracy of the DRG data.

This type of study [48] was performed in two different French districts (Côte d'Or and Doubs), including 18 public and private hospitals and two population-based cancer registries.

In this study, the main reason for false positives was prevalent cases. False negatives mainly concerned patients who did not receive care during the year of the diagnosis (time gap between diagnosis and hospitalisation or patients who were never hospitalised for their cancer). False negative also concerned a large number of patients who were treated, but who were not recorded in DRG database: this may be particularly due to coding errors in discharge abstracts collected in the DRG data source or a lack of exhaustiveness. This study also confirmed the inter-district variation and the influence of age on sensitivity and positive predictive values.

Different models were proposed. They all relied on the modeling of incidence in districts covered by registries. The parameters estimated in those models can then be used to estimate incidence at a national level.

The first approach relies on modeling of the ratio between incidence and cases identified in the DRG database. Regarding thyroid cancer, Uhry et al. [11] proposed using the ratio between incidence and hospital-based incidence in regions covered by registries in order to produce national and district-level estimations of thyroid cancer incidence in France. For each sex, the number of incident cases were analysed according to the number of surgery admissions using a Poisson regression, with age introduced as categorical fixed effect and district as random effect. The model's ability to predict incidence was tested through cross-validation by comparing the estimated incidence with the observed incidence by the registry, for each district covered by a registry.

In this study, the observed difference between the total number of observed and predicted cases through the 13 districts covered by a registry may be considered very low (30 out of 2049 predicted cases) which represents a relative error of 1.5 %. However, for each district, the relative error was often quite high and varied between –25% and +126%. One may wonder if the balance of the relative errors among the 13 districts can be extrapolated to the national level. Moreover, the authors could not link the anonymous national DRG database with the registry data and so determine in detail the reasons for the discordance between predicted (thanks to national DRG data) and observed (thanks to district registries) incidence, between 1998 and 2000.

The second approach is based on a logistic regression model [49]. The objective of this study is to develop and evaluate a method to ascertain a newly diagnosed breast cancer case using multiple sources of diagnoses and procedures from the Medicare claims system. Predictors of an incident case are operationally defined as codes for breast cancer-related diagnoses and procedures. The combination of predictors is then determined from a logistic regression analysis that includes predictors from the year of diagnosis as well as 2 years prior to diagnosis to eliminate prevalent cases. The optimal combination of predictors of a cancer case could be chosen thanks to the application to cases obtained from the linked SEER registries-Medicare claims database and a sample of non-cancer controls dawn from the SEER areas. This approach can produce higher levels of sensitivity (90%) and specificity (99.86%) than methods exclusively based on the identification of the diagnosis and surgical procedure codes that are known to produce low sensitivity (62%) [71].

However, this model has several limitations. Although it can produce high levels of sensitivity and specificity, the positive predictive value is comparatively low especially when the cancer incidence is low. Moreover, the stability of the estimated parameters in the model over a given time period may not be generalized to other time periods or other geographical areas. The relative weights of claims information can change with shifts in care practices as would occur, for example, if outpatient services or adjuvant therapy for older people were increased. Another limitation is that the model has to take into account different samples. A registry sample that contains incident cases and a control sample from the general population that has never been diagnosed as a cancer case.

3.2.3.3. Capture Recapture Method for Incidence Estimations

When there is no gold standard, such as cancer registries, that can list all incident cancer cases of the studied population, it is however possible to use the capture-recapture [50, 73, 74] method. This method requires data from at least two independent sources. Using information provided by duplicate cases (cases found in more than one source), an estimate of the number of individuals not identified can be calculated. From this number, the total number of incident cases (in a defined population) can be estimated. For example, some authors suggested using this method to estimate thyroid cancer incidence from two sources (DRG data and anatomopathological data [75]. However, this method has to respect certain conditions: the existence of independent sources (dependence between different sources can be taken account if there are more than 2 sources), each individual must have the same chance of being included in each source.

4. DISCUSSION

In this treatise, we have pointed out the advantages of using hospital discharge data to estimate cancer incidence [15] which rely on their availability, both at the national level and where cancer registries do not exist. They provide coded, structured and standardized personal medical data, accurately validated for financial reasons.

However, as stated, it is not possible to use a DRG database as the unique source of data to estimate the national incidence of cancer for several reasons. The inter-district variability in DRG data quality appears to be an important one. The improvement in the quality of DRG data over time also has to be considered. Such improvements are a significant source of variability, not only regarding the variability of one source over time, but also because improvements are not consistent in terms of time and space, *i.e.* not continuous and greater in some countries than in others, and they vary according to changes/differences in financial processes. As a consequence, it is necessary to regularly evaluate the quality of discharge data in districts covered by registries, using registry data as a gold standard for the validation of incidence estimated from DRG data, before extrapolating DRG data to estimate cancer incidence at a national level for the corresponding period. Statistical models need to be developed for another kind of variability, due to sociodemographic factors such as age, gender, period or geographical factors (migration, urban or rural). Further research is also needed to propose new algorithms, for example by combining already published algorithms to take advantage of the high level of specificity obtained in some (such as those relying on major surgical procedures) and of sensitivity obtained in others (relying only on diagnoses).

Though DRG databases cannot be used as a unique source to estimate cancer incidence, they are of great interest to epidemiologists for many purposes. For example, DRG databases could be an important source of data for descriptive cancer epidemiology used by registries to detect patients cared for outside their own areas (in a neighbouring district), and for cancer without a histological diagnosis. DRG data can also be used to estimate and analyse geographical variations in the use of health services for cancer at the national level, as they take into account variations in treatment practices [39]. This information is not always available in data from cancer registries.

Another important perspective for epidemiologists is increasing possibility of inter source linkage of very large national databases to provide information, such as individuals' socio-economic status or mortality, which is often missing in current health databases.

To reach this goal, many challenges, not only technical or financial, but also with regard to the requirements of privacy legislation, have to be overcome,.

The increasing power of informatics, the possibility to constitute huge databases, and the risk that they might be used without the agreement of the individuals whose data is stored are major concerns and legitimate fears for the population. The positive side of this technical efficiency is the development of powerful knowledge tools, which can potentially improve health policies. The negative aspect is the possible threat to privacy. Laws have provided protection for those concerns. Though health professionals, researchers and statisticians share the same concerns from an ethical point of view, these laws have restricted their activities. Such laws include the European directive of 24 October 1995 relative to the protection of persons in "the processing of personal data" which had to be incorporated into the internal laws of European member states. As a consequence, in many European countries, the legal restrictions concerning use of the national identity number for data access can make it impossible to link data from surveys with national health and socio-economic databases.

The development of appropriate methodologies has been another avenue of research. Secure linkage techniques [67, 68, 76] rely on irreversible encryption or hashing methods, applied to personal identifiers: a unique national identity number for example, or several identifying elements such as names, date or place of birth, address, etc., which are already present in the databases. In case of several identifiers, probabilistic linkage techniques can be applied to account for possible errors in data collection, even when the data are rendered anonymous.

As current health databases do not provide information regarding individual's socio-economic status, another major challenge would be to implement a handy way to incorporate such data. Linkage between health and socio-economic databases, (*e.g.* with national pension funds or insurance databases, with mortality data *etc*) would help to overcome these current drawbacks.

ACKNOWLEDGMENTS

We thank Philip Bastable for reviewing the English.

REFERENCES

[1] Kimberly JR, De Pouvourville G, D'Aunno T, editors. The globalization of managerial innovation in health care. Cambridge2008.

[2] Proceedings of the 24th International PCS/I Working Conference "Casemix beyond funding contributions for health policy"; 2008; Lisbon.

[3] Patient classification systems international:2009 Case Mix Conference. 5 november 2009; BMC Health Services Research2009. p. A20.

[4] Puukka E, Stehr-Green P, Becker TM. Measuring the health status gap for American Indians/Alaska Natives: getting closer to the truth. *Am J Public Health*, 2005 May;95(5):838-43.

[5] Ferlay J, Shin HR, Bray F, Forman D, Mathers C, Parkin DM. GLOBOCAN 2008, cancer incidence and mortality worldwide. *IARC CancerBase*, 2010(10).

[6] Hemminki K, Ji J, Brandt A, Mousavi SM, Sundquist J. The Swedish Family-Cancer Database 2009: prospects for histology-specific and immigrant studies. *Int J Cancer May*, 15;126(10):2259-67.

[7] Curado M, Edwards B, Shin H, all. e. Cancer incidence in Five Continents, 2007.

[8] Belot A, Grosclaude P, Bossard N, Jougla E, Benhamou E, Delafosse P, et al. Cancer incidence and mortality in France over the period 1980-2005. *Rev Epidemiol Sante Publique*, 2008 Jun;56(3):159-75.

[9] Tubiana M. [Trends in cancer mortality]. *Bull Cancer*, 1991;78(5):401-3.

[10] Powell J. Cancer registration: principles and methods. Data sources and reporting. *IARC Sci Publ.* 1991(95):29-42.

[11] Uhry Z, Colonna M, Remontet L, Grosclaude P, Carre N, Couris CM, et al. Estimating infra-national and national thyroid cancer incidence in France from cancer registries data and national hospital discharge database. *Eur J Epidemiol.* 2007;22(9):607-14.

[12] Remontet L, Mitton N, Couris CM, Iwaz J, Gomez F, Olive F, et al. Is it possible to estimate the incidence of breast cancer from medico-administrative databases? *Eur J Epidemiol.* 2008;23(10):681-8.

[13] Couris CM, Polazzi S, Olive F, Remontet L, Bossard N, Gomez F, et al. Breast cancer incidence using administrative data: correction with sensitivity and specificity. *J Clin Epidemiol.* 2009 Jun;62(6):660-6.

[14] Ganry O, Taleb A, Peng J, Raverdy N, Dubreuil A. Evaluation of an algorithm to identify incident breast cancer cases using DRGs data. *Eur J Cancer Prev.* 2003 Aug;12(4):295-9.

[15] McBean AM, Warren JL, Babish JD. Measuring the incidence of cancer in elderly Americans using Medicare claims data. *Cancer*, 1994 May 1;73(9):2417-25.

[16] Remy V, Mathevet P, Vainchtock A. Vulvar and vaginal cancers and dysplasia in France--an analysis of the hospital medical information system (PMSI) database. *Eur J Obstet Gynecol Reprod Biol.* 2009 Dec;147(2):210-4.

[17] Baldi I, Vicari P, Di Cuonzo D, Zanetti R, Pagano E, Rosato R, et al. A high positive predictive value algorithm using hospital administrative data identified incident cancer cases. *J Clin Epidemiol.* 2008 Apr;61(4):373-9.

[18] Wang PS, Walker AM, Tsuang MT, Orav EJ, Levin R, Avorn J. Finding incident breast cancer cases through US claims data and a state cancer registry. *Cancer Causes Control*, 2001 Apr;12(3):257-65.

[19] Goldberg M. [Administrative data bases: could they be useful for epidemiology?]. Rev Epidemiol Sante Publique2006 Sep;54(4):297-303.

[20] McKenzie K, Enraght-Moony EL, Walker SM, McClure RJ, Harrison JE. Accuracy of external cause-of-injury coding in hospital records. *Inj Prev*. 2009 Feb;15(1):60-4.

[21] Misset B, Nakache D, Vesin A, Darmon M, Garrouste-Orgeas M, Mourvillier B, et al. Reliability of diagnostic coding in intensive care patients. *Crit Care*, 2008;12(4):R95.

[22] Lain SJ, Roberts CL, Hadfield RM, Bell JC, Morris JM. How accurate is the reporting of obstetric haemorrhage in hospital discharge data? A validation study. *Aust N Z J Obstet Gynaecol*. 2008 Oct;48(5):481-4.

[23] Lloyd SS, Rissing JP. Physician and coding errors in patient records. *JAMA*, 1985 Sep 13;254(10):1330-6.

[24] Dixon J, Sanderson C, Elliott P, Walls P, Jones J, Petticrew M. Assessment of the reproducibility of clinical coding in routinely collected hospital activity data: a study in two hospitals. *J Public Health Med*. 1998 Mar;20(1):63-9.

[25] Humphries KH, Rankin JM, Carere RG, Buller CE, Kiely FM, Spinelli JJ. Co-morbidity data in outcomes research: are clinical data derived from administrative databases a reliable alternative to chart review? *J Clin Epidemiol*. 2000 Apr;53(4):343-9.

[26] Mahonen M, Salomaa V, Keskimaki I, Moltchanov V, Torppa J, Molarius A, et al. The feasibility of combining data from routine Hospital Discharge and Causes-of-Death Registers for epidemiological studies on stroke. *Eur J Epidemiol*. 2000;16(9):815-7.

[27] Quan H, Parsons GA, Ghali WA. Assessing accuracy of diagnosis-type indicators for flagging complications in administrative data. *J Clin Epidemiol*. 2004 Apr;57(4):366-72.

[28] Hsia DC, Krushat WM, Fagan AB, Tebbutt JA, Kusserow RP. Accuracy of diagnostic coding for Medicare patients under the prospective-payment system. *N Engl J Med*. 1988 Feb 11;318(6):352-5.

[29] Fisher ES, Whaley FS, Krushat WM, Malenka DJ, Fleming C, Baron JA, et al. The accuracy of Medicare's hospital claims data: progress has been made, but problems remain. *Am J Public Health*, 1992 Feb;82(2):243-8.

[30] Leppala JM, Virtamo J, Heinonen OP. Validation of stroke diagnosis in the National Hospital Discharge Register and the Register of Causes of Death in Finland. *Eur J Epidemiol*. 1999 Feb;15(2):155-60.

[31] Geller SE, Ahmed S, Brown ML, Cox SM, Rosenberg D, Kilpatrick SJ. International Classification of Diseases-9th revision coding for

preeclampsia: how accurate is it? *Am J Obstet Gynecol.* 2004 Jun;190(6):1629-33; discussion 33-4.
[32] Taylor LK, Travis S, Pym M, Olive E, Henderson-Smart DJ. How useful are hospital morbidity data for monitoring conditions occurring in the perinatal period? *Aust N Z J Obstet Gynaecol.* 2005 Feb;45(1):36-41.
[33] Lydon-Rochelle MT, Holt VL, Cardenas V, Nelson JC, Easterling TR, Gardella C, et al. The reporting of pre-existing maternal medical conditions and complications of pregnancy on birth certificates and in hospital discharge data. *Am J Obstet Gynecol.* 2005 Jul;193(1):125-34.
[34] Yasmeen S, Romano PS, Schembri ME, Keyzer JM, Gilbert WM. Accuracy of obstetric diagnoses and procedures in hospital discharge data. *Am J Obstet Gynecol.* 2006 Apr;194(4):992-1001.
[35] Henderson T, Shepheard J, Sundararajan V. Quality of diagnosis and procedure coding in ICD-10 administrative data. *Med Care*, 2006 Nov;44(11):1011-9.
[36] Peabody JW, Luck J, Jain S, Bertenthal D, Glassman P. Assessing the accuracy of administrative data in health information systems. *Med Care*, 2004 Nov;42(11):1066-72.
[37] Carre N, Uhry Z, Velten M, Tretarre B, Schvartz C, Molinie F, et al. [Predictive value and sensibility of hospital discharge system (PMSI) compared to cancer registries for thyroid cancer (1999-2000)]. *Rev Epidemiol Sante Publique*, 2006 Sep;54(4):367-76.
[38] Couris CM, Foret-Dodelin C, Rabilloud M, Colin C, Bobin JY, Dargent D, et al. [Sensitivity and specificity of two methods used to identify incident breast cancer in specialized units using claims databases]. *Rev Epidemiol Sante Publique*, 2004 Apr;52(2):151-60.
[39] Trombert Paviot B, Martin C, Vercherin P, all. e, editors. From case mix data bases to health geography. . In : Proceedings of the 19th International PCS/E Working Conference, Washington; 2003.
[40] Hadfield RM, Lain SJ, Cameron CA, Bell JC, Morris JM, Roberts CL. The prevalence of maternal medical conditions during pregnancy and a validation of their reporting in hospital discharge data. *Aust N Z J Obstet Gynaecol.* 2008 Feb;48(1):78-82.
[41] Klemmensen AK, Olsen SF, Osterdal ML, Tabor A. Validity of preeclampsia-related diagnoses recorded in a national hospital registry and in a postpartum interview of the women. *Am J Epidemiol.* 2007 Jul 15;166(2):117-24.

[42] Kahn EB, Berg CJ, Callaghan WM. Cesarean delivery among women with low-risk pregnancies: a comparison of birth certificates and hospital discharge data. *Obstet Gynecol.* 2009 Jan;113(1):33-40.
[43] Casez P, Labarere J, Sevestre MA, Haddouche M, Courtois X, Mercier S, et al. ICD-10 hospital discharge diagnosis codes were sensitive for identifying pulmonary embolism but not deep vein thrombosis. *J Clin Epidemiol.* Jul;63(7):790-7.
[44] Hasan M, Meara RJ, Bhowmick BK. The quality of diagnostic coding in cerebrovascular disease. *Int J Qual Health Care*, 1995 Dec;7(4):407-10.
[45] McBean AM, Babish JD, Warren JL. Determination of lung cancer incidence in the elderly using Medicare claims data. *Am J Epidemiol.* 1993 Jan 15;137(2):226-34.
[46] McClish DK, Penberthy L, Whittemore M, Newschaffer C, Woolard D, Desch CE, et al. Ability of Medicare claims data and cancer registries to identify cancer cases and treatment. *Am J Epidemiol.* 1997 Feb 1;145(3):227-33.
[47] Couris CM, Seigneurin A, Bouzbid S, Rabilloud M, Perrin P, Martin X, et al. French claims data as a source of information to describe cancer incidence: predictive values of two identification methods of incident prostate cancers. *J Med Syst.* 2006 Dec;30(6):459-63.
[48] Quantin C, Benzenine E, Fassa M, Hägi M, Fournier E, Gentil J, et al. Evaluation of the interest of using discharge abstract databases to estimate breast cancer incidence in two french departments. IJOS2010.
[49] Freeman JL, Zhang D, Freeman DH, Goodwin JS. An approach to identifying incident breast cancer cases using Medicare claims data. *J Clin Epidemiol.* 2000 Jun;53(6):605-14.
[50] Hafdi-Nejjari Z, Couris CM, Schott AM, Perrot L, Bourgoin F, Borson-Chazot F, et al. [Role of hospital claims databases from care units for estimating thyroid cancer incidence in the Rhone-Alpes region of France]. *Rev Epidemiol Sante Publique*, 2006 Oct;54(5):391-8.
[51] Koroukian SM, Cooper GS, Rimm AA. Ability of Medicaid claims data to identify incident cases of breast cancer in the Ohio Medicaid population. *Health Serv Res.* 2003 Jun;38(3):947-60.
[52] Leung KM, Hasan AG, Rees KS, Parker RG, Legorreta AP. Patients with newly diagnosed carcinoma of the breast: validation of a claim-based identification algorithm. *J Clin Epidemiol.* 1999 Jan;52(1):57-64.
[53] Uhry Z, Remontet L, Grosclaude P, Velten M, Colonna M. [Estimating the incidence of colorectal cancer in France from a hospital discharge

database, 1999-2003]. *Rev Epidemiol Sante Publique*, 2009 Oct;57(5):329-36.

[54] Fisher ES, Baron JA, Malenka DJ, Barrett J, Bubolz TA. Overcoming potential pitfalls in the use of Medicare data for epidemiologic research. *Am J Public Health*, 1990 Dec;80(12):1487-90.

[55] Haynes K, Forde KA, Schinnar R, Wong P, Strom BL, Lewis JD. Cancer incidence in The Health Improvement Network. *Pharmacoepidemiol Drug Saf.* 2009 Aug;18(8):730-6.

[56] 56.   Hamilton W, Lancashire R, Sharp D, Peters TJ, Cheng KK, Marshall T. The importance of anaemia in diagnosing colorectal cancer: a case-control study using electronic primary care records. *Br J Cancer*, 2008 Jan 29;98(2):323-7.

[57] Jensen AR, Overgaard J, Storm HH. Validity of breast cancer in the Danish Cancer Registry. A study based on clinical records from one county in Denmark. *Eur J Cancer Prev.* 2002 Aug;11(4):359-64.

[58] Potosky AL, Riley GF, Lubitz JD, Mentnech RM, Kessler LG. Potential for cancer related health services research using a linked Medicare-tumor registry database. *Med Care*, 1993 Aug;31(8):732-48.

[59] Freeman JL, Klabunde CN, Schussler N, Warren JL, Virnig BA, Cooper GS. Measuring breast, colorectal, and prostate cancer screening with medicare claims data. *Med Care*, 2002 Aug;40(8 Suppl):IV-36-42.

[60] Cooper GS, Virnig B, Klabunde CN, Schussler N, Freeman J, Warren JL. Use of SEER-Medicare data for measuring cancer surgery. *Med Care*, 2002 Aug;40(8 Suppl):IV-43-8.

[61] Du X, Freeman JL, Warren JL, Nattinger AB, Zhang D, Goodwin JS. Accuracy and completeness of Medicare claims data for surgical treatment of breast cancer. *Med Care*, 2000 Jul;38(7):719-27.

[62] Virnig BA, Warren JL, Cooper GS, Klabunde CN, Schussler N, Freeman J. Studying radiation therapy using SEER-Medicare-linked data. *Med Care*, 2002 Aug;40(8 Suppl):IV-49-54.

[63] Warren JL, Harlan LC, Fahey A, Virnig BA, Freeman JL, Klabunde CN, et al. Utility of the SEER-Medicare data to identify chemotherapy use. *Med Care*, 2002 Aug;40(8 Suppl):IV-55-61.

[64] Potosky AL, Warren JL, Riedel ER, Klabunde CN, Earle CC, Begg CB. Measuring complications of cancer treatment using the SEER-Medicare data. *Med Care*, 2002 Aug;40(8 Suppl):IV-62-8.

[65] Goodwin JS, Zhang DD, Ostir GV. Effect of depression on diagnosis, treatment, and survival of older women with breast cancer. *J Am Geriatr Soc*. 2004 Jan;52(1):106-11.

[66] Lackan NA, Ostir GV, Freeman JL, Mahnken JD, Goodwin JS. Decreasing variation in the use of hospice among older adults with breast, colorectal, lung, and prostate cancer. *Med Care*, 2004 Feb;42(2):116-22.

[67] Quantin C, Binquet C, Allaert FA, Cornet B, Pattisina R, Leteuff G, et al. Decision analysis for the assessment of a record linkage procedure: application to a perinatal network. *Methods Inf Med*. 2005;44(1):72-9.

[68] Quantin C, Bouzelat H, Allaert FA, Benhamiche AM, Faivre J, Dusserre L. How to ensure data security of an epidemiological follow-up: quality assessment of an anonymous record linkage procedure. *Int J Med Inform*. 1998 Mar;49(1):117-22.

[69] Jaro MA. Probabilistic linkage of large public health data files. *Stat Med*. 1995 Mar 15-Apr 15;14(5-7):491-8.

[70] Cooper GS, Yuan Z, Stange KC, Dennis LK, Amini SB, Rimm AA. The sensitivity of Medicare claims data for case ascertainment of six common cancers. *Med Care*, 1999 May;37(5):436-44.

[71] Warren JL, Feuer E, Potosky AL, Riley GF, Lynch CF. Use of Medicare hospital and physician data to assess breast cancer incidence. *Med Care*, 1999 May;37(5):445-56.

[72] Couris CM, Colin C, Rabilloud M, Schott AM, Ecochard R. Method of correction to assess the number of hospitalized incident breast cancer cases based on claims databases. J Clin Epidemiol2002 Apr;55(4):386-91.

[73] Laporte RE. Assessing the human condition: capture-recapture techniques. *BMJ*, 1994 Jan 1;308(6920):5-6.

[74] McCarty DJ, Tull ES, Moy CS, Kwoh CK, LaPorte RE. Ascertainment corrected rates: applications of capture-recapture methods. *Int J Epidemiol*. 1993 Jun;22(3):559-65.

[75] Ismail AA, Beeching NJ, Gill GV, Bellis MA. How many data sources are needed to determine diabetes prevalence by capture-recapture? *Int J Epidemiol*. 2000 Jun;29(3):536-41.

[76] Quantin C, Fassa M, Coatrieux G, Trouessin G, Allaert FA. Combining hashing and enciphering algorithms for epidemiological analysis of gathered data. *Methods Inf Med*. 2008;47(5):454-8.

In: Data Collection and Storage
Editor: Julian R. Eiras

ISBN 978-1-61209-689-6
© 2012 Nova Science Publishers, Inc.

Chapter 2

MULTIPLEXING HOLOGRAMS FOR DATA PAGE STORAGE

Elena Fernandez Varó[1], Manuel Pérez Molina[2], Rosa Fuentes Rosillo[1], Celia García Llopis[1], Augusto Beléndez Vázquez[2], and Inmaculada Pascual Villalobos[1]

[1] Dep. Óptica, Farmacología y Anatomía, Universidad de Alicante, Spain
[2] Dep. Física, Ingeniería de Sistemas y Teoría de la Señal, Universidad de Alicante, Spain

ABSTRACT

We live in an age of information science and new technologies in which the use of computers, music players, and video or data storage memory for information processing and storage has become essential. The conventional optical memory technologies, like CD-ROMs and DVDs, are two-dimensional surface-storage techniques, and thus have almost arrived at the limit of their capacity and are becoming obsolete. This fact has given rise to many researchers in the world focusing on new techniques to design devices with larger storage capacity such as holographic storage devices. These devices can store the entire volume of the informational material thereby increasing storage capacity compared with 2D that can only store the information on the surface.

In order to manufacture a holographic data storage device it is necessary to get the maximum number of holograms in the recording material. Therefore, it is necessary to study the different techniques that allow multiplexing a large number of holograms on the material. The information to be stored is introduced through liquid crystal displays, (LCD). These devices have been extensively studied for use as spatial light modulators (SLM) due to their ability to modify, in real time, both the amplitude and phase of the incident light. In particular, data pages are sent to the LCD and their spatial frequencies are recorded in the material.

Binary intensity modulation is commonly used to encrypt the information sent to the LCD. However, this type of modulation produces a high zero frequency with an intensity several orders of magnitude higher than other frequencies. As a result, the dynamic range of the material is saturated, limiting the storage capacity.

The problems caused by the lack of homogeneity at the spectrum can be solved by using some other modulation schemes, such as random phase masks, binary π radians phase-only modulation (πBPM), full multi-phase scheme or hybrid ternary modulation (HTM).

The study proposed in this abstract combines the basic elements needed for a realistic realization of a holographic data storage system: the recording material, the codification scheme for the data pages, and the multiplexing methodology.

INTRODUCTION

We live in the age of information science and new technologies, in which the use of computers music players, video, and data storage memory for information processing and storage has become something quotidian. The users of these technologies store large amounts of digital data. In addition, huge amounts of data on the banks, companies, or government archives are stored on devices that occupy a large space, which could be reduced if the devices had a higher storage capacity per unit volume. Conventional optical memory technologies like CD-ROMs and DVDs are two-dimensional surface-storage techniques, and thus they have almost reached the limit of their capacity and become obsolete. This fact has encouraged world researchers to focus on new techniques to design devices with larger storage capacity, as it is the case of holographic storage devices. These devices can store the entire volume of the informational material thereby increasing the storage capacity in comparison with two-dimensional devices that only store the information on the surface. Companies such as Bayer and InPhase came together to create the Tapestry^{TM} [1,2], the first prototype of a holographic optical storage system that is being used by leading companies and is capable of storing 200 Gbytes to 1.6 Tbytes in a disk 130 mm of diameter.

The manufacture of a holographic data storage device requires getting the maximum number of holograms in a recording material, so it is necessary to study the different techniques that allow multiplexing a large number of holograms on the material. The information to be stored is introduced through Liquid Crystal Displays (LCD) [3-6], which have been extensively studied to be used as spatial light modulators (SLM) for their ability to modify in real time the amplitude and phase of the incident light. In particular, data pages are sent to the LCD and their spatial frequencies are recorded in the material, commonly using binary intensity modulation to encrypt the information sent to the LCD. However, this type of modulation gives rise to a high peak at zero frequency (d. c. component) whose intensity is several orders of magnitude higher than the rest of frequencies [7]. Because of this zero frequency peak, the dynamic range of the material is saturated and therefore the storage capacity is constrained.

The problems caused by the lack of homogeneity in the spectrum can be solved by using other modulation schemes different to the binary one, such as random phase masks [8], binary π radians phase-only modulation (πBPM) [9-12], full multi-phase scheme [13,14] or hybrid ternary modulation (HTM) [10,12,15-17]. The study proposed in this chapter combines the basic elements required for a realistic fabrication of a holographic data storage system: the recording material, the codification scheme for the data pages and the multiplexing methodology.

1. HOLOGRAPHIC MULTIPLEXING GRATINGS

To manufacture holographic memory considerations must be taken into account to achieve the maximum storage capacity of digital information. The first consideration is the storage of multiple gratings, which requires suitable materials with high storage capacity. These materials must have large thickness (about 1 mm), high sensitivity, and their selectivity angular energy must be as small as possible, thereby allowing them to obtain high values for the dynamic range [18]. The second consideration is the amount of stored information, which is the maximum number of bits/μm^2. In this sense, it is necessary to use the holographic multiplexing techniques that allow storage of the largest number of holograms in the same position of the material [19-

21]. Thirdly, all the holograms to be stored must have the same diffraction efficiency, which is needed to better exploit the dynamic range of the material and to store more holograms achieving higher diffraction efficiencies. For this reason, we will use a recording method to calculate the exposure time for each of the holograms to achieve equal diffraction efficiencies [22].

1.1. Experimental Setup

The experimental setup used for recording holographic diffraction gratings is shown in Figure 1. The laser used in the recording stage is an Nd: YVO4 (Coherent Verdi V2) that emits a beam of light with a wavelength of 532 nm, at which the material is sensitive. The laser used in the reconstruction stage is a He-Ne laser at 633 nm, wavelength at which the material is not sensitive.

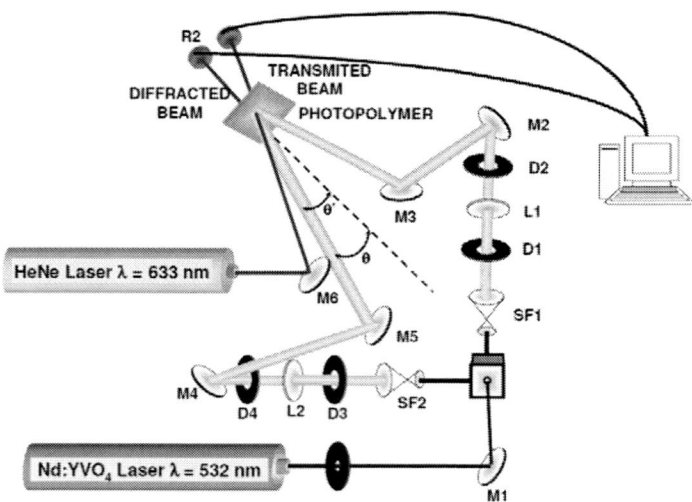

Figure 1. Holographic Setup. Me: mirrors, BS: beam splitter, Li: lens, SFi: A set of spatial filter and microscope objective, Di: diaphragm, Ri: radiometers.

In the registration stage, two coherent beams named object beam and reference beam overlap in the material to form the hologram (in this section both beams will be regarded as plane waves, so the resulting interference pattern will be a diffraction grating). These two beams are the result of splitting the beam emitted by the laser by means of a beam splitter, and each of them passes through a microscope objective and a pinhole to be expanded and filtered respectively. Then each beam passes through a series of lenses and diaphragms that collimate them with the desired diameter, and finally, the beams are directed to the material with the desired angle through a series of mirrors.

1.2. Multiplexing Methods

The hologram multiplexing consists of storing multiple holograms without overlapping in a given position of the material. The best way to optimize the entire volume of the holographic material is to combine different methods to store all multiplexed holograms allowed by the material avoiding the overlapping between different holograms. Different hologram multiplexing methods can be found in the literature [23]:

a) Angular multiplexing in plane: The reference beam is a plane wave and the multiplexing occurs when varying the angle of incidence of reference beam, being the latter is always in the same plane as the object beam [24].
b) Angular multiplexing out of plane: It is similar to the previous method, but here the reference beam is in the plane normal to the optical axis defined by the object beam.
c) Peristrophic multiplexing: The reference beam is a plane wave, and the object and reference beams overlap on the material forming a certain angle. The multiplexing occurs when spinning the material with respect to a rotation axis perpendicular [22,25] or parallel [18,19,26] to its surface.
d) Wavelength multiplexing: The reference beam is a plane wave and the multiplexing mechanism is the change in the wavelength of the reference beam [22,27,28].
e) Phase code multiplexing: The reference beam is a plane wave modulated in one dimension by a spatial light modulator. The dimension that is modulated is the plane defined by the optical axis of the object beam and the reference beam [8].
f) Shift multiplexing in plane: The reference beam is a spherical wave and the mechanism of multiplexing is based on the location of holographic media with respect to the reference beam. [29].

g) <u>Shift multiplexing out of plane:</u> The reference beam is a spherical wave that is in the plane normal to the optical axis defined by the object beam and its projection on the surface of the recording material.

h) <u>Spatial multiplexing:</u> The object and reference beams impinge on the material in different spatial positions for the different holograms.

1.3. Recording Material

The main feature of a good holographic recording material is the ability to modify some of its optical properties, such as the absorption coefficient, the thickness or the refractive index [30] by exposing it to light, preferably with a linear response for the previous properties with respect to light exposure. In addition, these materials must have a high resolution, since the separation between the interference fringes is usually of the order of 1 μm or less. Another aspect to be considered is the range of wavelengths absorbed by the material, since the recording wavelength of the laser must lie within this range so that hologram recording is achievable. In addition, these materials must also have high-energy sensitivity, low noise, low absorption losses, stability during the recording of hologram and, they must be reusable and/or as cheap as possible.

Different types of recording material with some the aforementioned properties have been investigated, as in the case of photographic emulsions, photochromic materials, the photoresist, photothermoplastic materials, dichromated gelatin, gelatin silver halide sensitized, photopolymers, and photorefractive materials. Recently, many studies have focused on the manufacture and optimization of materials that can be used for holographic storage. Such materials can be either single-use (WORM, write one, read many) [18,31-36] or rewritable [36-38]. In addition, biodegradable materials are also being currently studied [39,40].

However, amongst these materials, we can highlight the photopolymer as the most versatile for several reasons: they allow the storage of holograms with high refractive index modulation and high optical quality, do not require development processes, have a low cost, and can easily vary their properties (such as energy sensitivity or spectral absorption rate) by simply changing its composition [18,31,41]. Besides, these materials can exhibit a high dynamic range depending on their thickness. The dynamic range M # is a parameter that describes the ability of a material, together with the experimental device, to store holograms [19,31,42]. In order to store the maximum amount of information in a holographic memory, the dynamic range is required to be as high as possible so that one can store the largest number of holograms in the same position and with the highest diffraction performance.

1.4. Angular Selectivity

An important parameter that must be measured is the angular selectivity of the holographic material, which defines the minimum angular separation distance between the holograms so that they do not overlap. In this chapter, the holograms are recorded using peristrophic multiplexing with respect to two rotation axes, one of them perpendicular to the material surface and the other one parallel to it, so the angular selectivity will be calculated with respect to both axes.

In the case of perpendicular peristrophic multiplexing, the method used to calculate the angular selectivity is described in references [23,25]. Because of the geometry of this type of multiplexing, in the reconstruction stage of one of the holograms, the diffracted beams from the rest of holograms also appear, but they are reconstructed at different angles. Consequently, the problem of measuring the angular selectivity reduces to calculate the angular size of the detector surface wherever it is placed and ensure that the holograms are stored with an angular separation greater than the angular size of the detector. The main advantage of perpendicular peristrophic multiplexing is that the calculation of the angular selectivity is purely geometrical and it can be modified by changing the size of the detector or the distance between the detector and the hologram.

In the case of parallel peristrophic multiplexing [43,44], the angular selectivity is defined as the angular bandwidth of the main lobe of the diffraction efficiency curve when it is plotted as a function of the reconstruction angle. In order to store multiple holograms without overlapping, it is necessary to measure the angular bandwidth of the main lobes for the different holograms to make sure that the angular spacing between such lobes is greater than their angular bandwidth. This kind of study achieves the maximum number of angular recording positions without overlapping in any of the holograms.

1.5. Dynamic Range

Another important parameter in the design of holographic data storage memories is the dynamic range [19,31,42]. The dynamic range is defined as the number of holograms with a diffraction efficiency $\eta = 1$ (100%) that can be stored in a material with a given thickness. Its mathematical expression is given by:

$$M\# = \sum_{i=1}^{N} \eta_i^{1/2} \qquad (1)$$

where η_i is the diffraction efficiency of each hologram, and N the number of recorded holograms.

To calculate the dynamic range we must sum the square roots of the diffraction efficiencies of all the holograms that have been recorded in the material, as it is shown in equation 1. From the dynamic range, it is possible to find out the number of holograms that could be stored in the material to obtain a certain diffraction efficiency or alternatively the average diffraction efficiency for a given number of stored holograms. This latter average efficiency is given by:

$$\eta_{AVR} = \left(\frac{M\#}{N}\right)^2 \qquad (2)$$

where N is the number of stored holograms.

1.6. Holographic Storage of Diffraction Gratings

Once the energy sensitivity of the material [45], the angular selectivity and dynamic range are defined, the next step is to store the diffraction gratings in the material. It is recommended that all holograms be stored with the same diffraction efficiency in order to avoid errors that may appear in the reading of the hologram because of too low diffraction efficiencies or due to the fact that the dynamic range is not distributed along all the holograms. For this purpose, the holograms are stored with uniform diffraction efficiencies by using the Schedule Exposure Method (SEM). This method calculates the optimal exposure times to make uniform the diffraction performance of all holograms, taking into account the diffraction efficiencies obtained by storing a number of holograms.

To fully exploit the dynamic range of the material it is necessary to store as many holograms as possible. In this study, 90 holograms are stored at the same location using a combination of perpendicular and parallel peristrophic multiplexing [46].

For the first hologram to be recorded, a specific exposure must be used taking into account that the material will not respond under lower exposures. For this reason, the first hologram is stored with an exposure time of 2 seconds. In order to store the other holograms, different configurations were tested previously. First, we stored all the holograms with the same exposure time, but the first holograms had high diffraction efficiencies and the last ones had diffraction efficiencies close to 0%. When the holograms are stored, the monomer and the dye are consumed and therefore the material becomes less sensitive. For this reason, it is necessary to increase the exposure time for the last holograms so that they reach the same diffraction efficiency as the first ones. Instead of storing all the holograms with the same exposure time, we decided to increase this time as the number of stored holograms increased. The exposure times that are used initially to store the holograms and that are chosen depending on the material are called "initial iteration times" in our study.

The exposure time used to store the holograms at the initial iteration is given as follows: 2 s for the first hologram (necessary time so that the material responds), 0.5 s for holograms 2 to 6, and for every additional five stored holograms we add 0.5 s [47]. Once the holograms have been stored with the exposure times of the initial iteration, the diffraction efficiency of each one of them is measured. Figure 2 represents with full circles the diffraction efficiency obtained with these exposure times, and it can be appreciated that the first holograms exhibit higher diffraction efficiency (around 2.5%) than the last holograms (around 0.02%). Therefore, for the holograms to be stored with uniform diffraction efficiency it is necessary to decrease the exposure times for the first holograms and increase the exposure times for the last ones. The SEM is used to calculate these exposure times, which are called "exposure times of first iteration".

From the diffraction efficiencies given in Figure 2, we calculated the cumulative grating strength,

$$\sum_{i=1}^{N} \eta_i^{1/2},$$

where η is the diffraction efficiency and N is the number of holograms stored so far. When the curve is saturated, we can obtain the dynamic range, which in this case is M# = 13.5.

In order to store our desired number of 90 holograms with uniform diffraction efficiency, the data obtained from Figure 2 are fitted according to the following theoretical equation:

$$A = a_0 + a_1E + a_2E^2 + a_3E^3 + a_4E^4 + a_5E^5 + a_6E^6 \quad (3)$$

where A is the cumulative grating strength and E the exposure energy. Once the coefficients a_i have been calculated, the time needed to record the holograms may be calculated from equation 4:

$$t_n = A_{Sat} \Bigg/ N \cdot I \Bigg[a_1 + 2a_2 \sum_{i=1}^{n-1} E_i + 3a_3 \left(\sum_{i=1}^{n-1} E_i \right)^2 + 4a_4 \left(\sum_{i=1}^{n-1} E_i \right)^3 + 5a_5 \left(\sum_{i=1}^{n-1} E_i \right)^4 + 6a_6 \left(\sum_{i=1}^{n-1} E_i \right)^5 \Bigg] \quad (4)$$

where A_{sat} is the obtained dynamic range, N is the number of holograms to be stored, I is the recording intensity, and E_i is the energy used to record up to the i-th hologram.

Figure 2 shows the exposures of the first iteration with empty triangles, which are obtained by fitting the cumulative grating strength according to equations 3 and 4. With these exposures, 90 holograms are stored again and the obtained diffraction efficiency obtained is depicted with empty squares in Figure 2.

After the first iteration, the obtained dynamic range is M# = 12, the mean diffraction efficiency is 2.1% and the diffraction efficiencies are much more uniform and closer to the average diffraction efficiency than the ones obtained with the initial iteration.

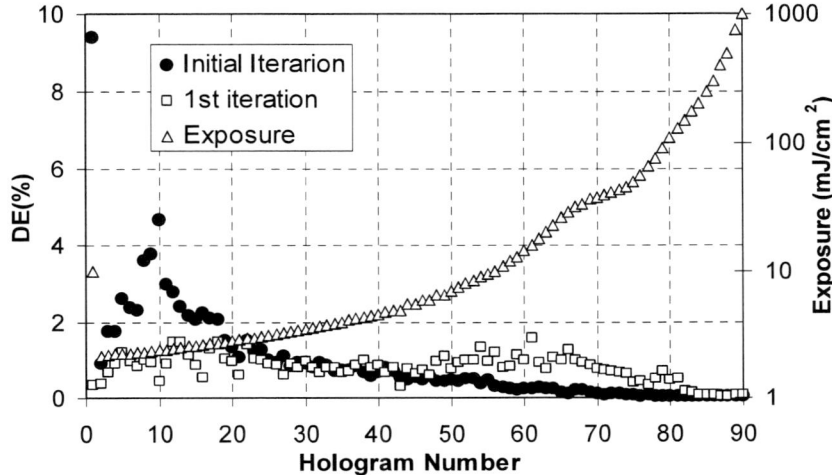

Figure 2. Diffraction efficiency versus hologram number for the initial iteration (full circles) and for the first iteration (empty squares) for a combination of peristrophic and angular multiplexing, and the exposure used to obtain them (empty triangles).

2. TWISTED-NEMATIC LIQUID CRYSTAL DISPLAYS FOR HOLOGRAPHIC DATA STORAGE

In the previous section, we considered the multiplexing of a large number of gratings, which is the first step to make a holographic storage memory. However, we need to store the information in a digital format made up of bits of information, so the next step is to replace the diffraction gratings by digital data pages that act as an object. The type of object used as a data page is composed of black and white squares to emulate the bits "one" and "zero" respectively. An LCD is used to send such binary objects to the object beam.

We must bear in mind that there are different ways of sending data pages to an LCD, that is, there are different ways to modulate the object beam in the holographic setup (which is what is stored in the material). Among the different modulations, the binary intensity modulation is one of the most frequently used due to its simplicity. In this type of modulation, the Fourier Transform (FT) of the data page is holographically recorded on a photosensitive material. However, this modulation gives rise to a large zero frequency peak, which may saturate the dynamic range of the material and thus limit the accessible dynamic range. The problems caused by the lack of homogeneity of the FT can be solved by using other different modulation schemes such as random phase masks [8], binary π radians phase-only modulation (πBPM) [9-12], full multi-phase scheme [13,14] or hybrid ternary modulation (HTM) [10,12,15-17].

In this section, we are going to describe how data pages were sent to the LCD and stored in the material using two different types of modulations: binary intensity modulation and hybrid ternary modulation. The main reason we use these two modulations is that we began our study using the binary intensity modulation and then we changed to the HTM because it allowed us to reduce the zero frequency peak using exactly the same experimental scheme as the one for the binary intensity modulation. This interesting feature of the HTM enabled us to compare the results of both modulations. The only difference between binary intensity modulation and the HTM is the type of codified object sent to the LCD, without any additional adjustments in the setup, which makes straightforward the implementation of this new scheme. In this sense, the use of other modulation schemes, such as full multi-phase modulation, involve interferometric methods in the reconstruction, which adds additional complexity to the experimental setup.

In the first step of our holographic recording process, the LCD together with a range of external elements of polarization (polarizers and retardation plate) are calibrated by changing the angle of the external elements of polarization to enable the LCD to behave as desired under certain constraints: as a light amplitude modulator, as a light phase modulator only, etc. Secondly, we optimize the LCD to obtain the suitable angles of the polarizers and retardation plate as well as the gray levels in order to carry out these two types of modulations. Finally, we compare the results obtained with the binary intensity modulation and HTM to see which of them would provide the best for the holographic data storage.

2.1. Characterization of the Spatial Light Modulator

Twisted-nematic liquid crystal displays (TN-LCDs) have been studied for their applications as spatial light modulators (SLMs), which are used to modify in real time the amplitude or phase of a light beam [3-6,17,48]. Some of the most important applications of the LCD are the design of programmable optical elements such as lenses [49] and diffraction gratings, as well as their applications for holographic data storage. In the case of holographic data storage, LCD can refresh the data page to be stored in the material in real time [50].

The LCD changes the polarization state of incident light. In order to control the polarization state at the output of LCD using it as an SLM, it is necessary to place the LCD between linear polarizers and, in general, it is necessary to include a retardant wave plate for calibration purposes [51]. Once the LCD is calibrated, it can modulate the light amplitude and/or phase as desired (with certain constraints) just by changing the angle of the external polarization elements. To achieve the aforementioned modes of operation for the LCD, it is necessary to calibrate the LCD and the polarizers and use the values obtained from the calibration to optimize the external elements and the LCD. This optimization consists of calculating the values of the angles that must be set in the external elements to achieve the desired polarization states. Extensive literature explaining LCD calibration and optimization has been written [4,6,51], so here we will provide with a brief explanation regarding the calibration process.

The calibration process consists of two steps. In the first step, the LCD is turned off and no voltage is applied. In this step, three parameters that are independent of the voltage are calculated: the total twist angle (α), the orientation of the molecular director at the input face (Ψ_D) and the maximum birefringence ($\beta_{max} = \pi d(n_e - n_o)/\lambda$, where d is the thickness of the LCD, n_e is the extraordinary refractive index, n_o is the ordinary refractive index and λ is the wavelength) [52,53]. In the second step, the parameters that depend on the voltage are measured. Such parameters are related to the variation of optical anisotropy properties throughout the thickness of the cell as a function of the applied voltage. This model attempts to take into account the fact that the liquid crystal molecules near the glass are almost completely adhered to its surface and cannot reorient themselves when the voltage is applied. Thus, the total thickness d of the LCD may be decomposed into two lateral regions of width d_1 and a central region of width d_2. In this way, the anisotropic properties of the LCD may be modelled using two voltage-dependent parameters – birefringence β and δ –, which can be expressed as:

$$\beta(V) = \pi \Delta n \, d_2 / \lambda_0$$
$$\delta(V) = \pi \Delta n_{max} d_1 / \lambda_0$$
(5)

where λ_0 is the beam wavelength, Δn is the difference between the ordinary and extraordinary index and Δn_{max} is the maximum value of Δn.

From the curves $\beta(V)$ and $\delta(V)$ we can find the angles at which the polarizers must be set in the experimental setup to modulate the incident beam. Depending on how the modulator is intended to act (intensity, phase or both), it will be necessary to set some different angles on these polarizers.

2.2. Optimization of the SLM to Obtain Modulations for Holographic Data Storage

Once the LCD is calibrated, the next step is its optimization. The optimization process consists of finding out the gray level values that must be sent to the LCD and the angles of the polarizers, which must be placed before and after the LCD to module the object beam, based on the calibrated birefringence and as a function of voltage applied to the LCD.

For binary intensity modulation it is necessary to find two states which meet the condition of maximum contrast, that is, a state with maximum intensity (white bits of the data page) and another one with low intensity (black bits). Once the adjustment is completed, Figure 3 shows the obtained transmittance values versus the gray level. These values have been obtained for an orientation of the transmission axes of the polarizers given by the angles $\varphi_1=116°$ and $\varphi_2=111°$ with respect to the laboratory reference system, where φ_1 corresponds to the polarizer placed in front of the LCD and φ_2 corresponds to the polarizer placed behind the LCD [6]. It has been found that the gray level that provides maximum transmittance is 250, whereas the gray level that provides the lowest transmittance is 0. With these two states, the system achieves a maximum contrast of 98%, where the contrast M is defined as $M = (I_{max} - I_{min})/(I_{max} + I_{min})$.

This is one of the modulation types that can be used for holographic data storage [54]. However, if the Fourier Transform (FT) is analyzed, we find that the zero order of the FT is several orders of magnitude more intense than the rest of frequencies, which does not help to optimize the dynamic range of the material or imply that the image quality is better. Consequently, this type of modulation would not be the most suitable for holographic data storage, since the zero order consumes the components of the material more quickly, limiting the number of holograms that can be stored.

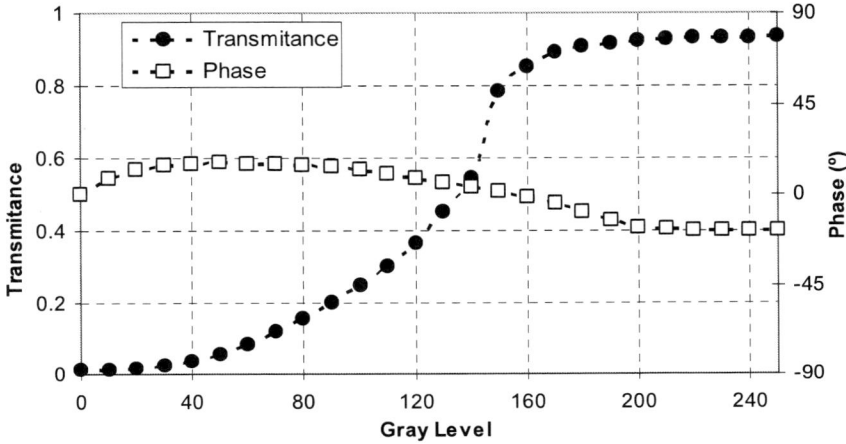

Figure 3. Transmittance and phase obtained in the optimization of the LCD to get a binary intensity modulation.

Figure 4. FT obtained with binary intensity modulation.

Figure 4 shows the FT of the data page obtained with the binary intensity modulation. The central area of the FT has been zoomed to appreciate it better. As shown, all the energy is concentrated in the FT zero order and no energy at other frequency components can be observed.

To prevent the zero-order to be so intense (which reduces the storage capacity of the material), people use other types of modulation that allow distributing the intensity among the other frequencies.

Some studies have chosen to blur the FT so that the zero order is not as intense compared to other frequencies, but this procedure is incompatible with the associative property of holographic memories. An alternative option is to use random phase masks to reduce the zero order [8]. Other methods to reduce the zero order consist of the use of a binary phase only modulation where the two states have a phase difference of π rad (πBPM) [7,9,11], or a method that combines the two types of modulation: hybrid ternary modulation amplitude and phase HTM [7,15-17].

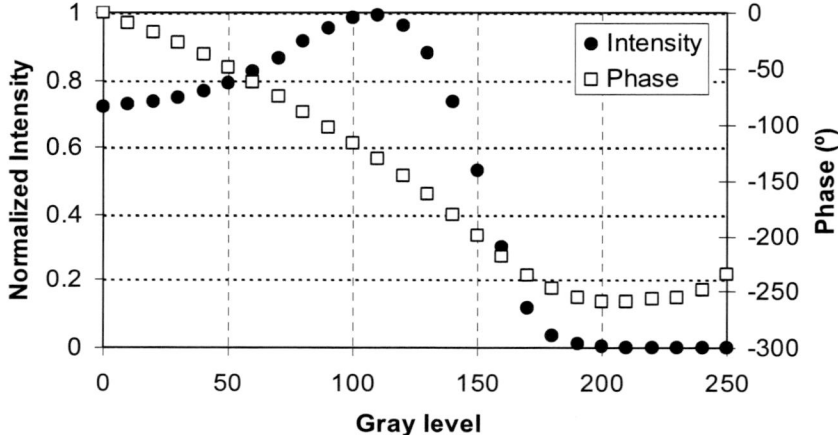

Figure 5. Transmittance and phase obtained in the optimization of the LCD to get the HTM.

In the case of HTM, it is necessary to find three states: two of them corresponding to the white bits with a phase difference of π rad and maximum transmittance, and a third state which corresponds to the black bits with minimum transmittance. After performing the optimization process [6], the obtained transmittance and phase are shown in Figure 5, whose values have been achieved by setting the polarizers at the angles $\varphi_1=134°$ and $\varphi_2=65°$. In this configuration, the two states of maximum transmittance and phase shift of 180 ° is obtained with the gray levels 0 and 140, while the state of minimum transmittance is obtained with the gray level 250. For these gray levels, the maximum contrast is 99% and the phase difference between the two states is 180°.

Figure 6 shows the FT that is obtained by sending an object generated with the three states required in the HTM and the bits chosen randomly. As it can be appreciated, all the frequencies are distributed across the Fourier plane.

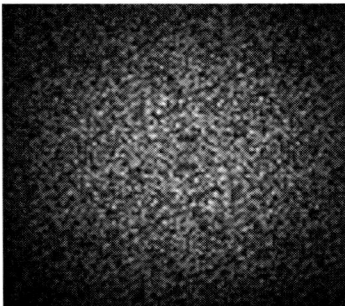

Figure 6. FT obtained with the HTM.

We can therefore conclude that the best modulation to manufacture holographic data memories is the HTM, since it gives a more uniform FT spectrum and thus allows better exploitation of the dynamic range of the holographic material.

2.3. Holographic Setup

In our experimental setup shown in Figure 7, the holographic data pages were stored using a Nd:YVO$_4$ laser (Coherent Verdi V2) with a wavelength of 532 nm, at which the material is sensitive. The polarized beam emitted by the laser was split into two beams with a beam-splitter. Each beam was expanded and filtered using a microscope objective and a pinhole. Then the beams passed through a series of lenses and diaphragms in order to obtain collimated beams with the desired diameter. The two laser beams were spatially overlapped at the recording medium.

The LCD was placed in the object beam between two polarizers and two quarter-wave plates, one in each side of the LCD. The LCD, polarizers, and quarter-wave plates were used as an SLM. In addition, a lens (L4) was placed in front of the SLM to perform the Fourier Transform (FT) of the data page, which was sent to the SLM.

A diaphragm is placed just in front of the photopolymer to block all the diffraction orders that emerge from the LCD except the central order. If the other orders were not blocked, then they would also be stored in the material and interference patterns would be observed on the image during reconstruction, thus worsening the image quality. The reference beam is a plane wave that interferes with the object beam at the material surface. In previous papers we studied how the beam ratio between the object and reference beams affects the quality of the stored images [55]. These beam intensities were measured at the position where the photopolymer must be placed when the holograms are stored.

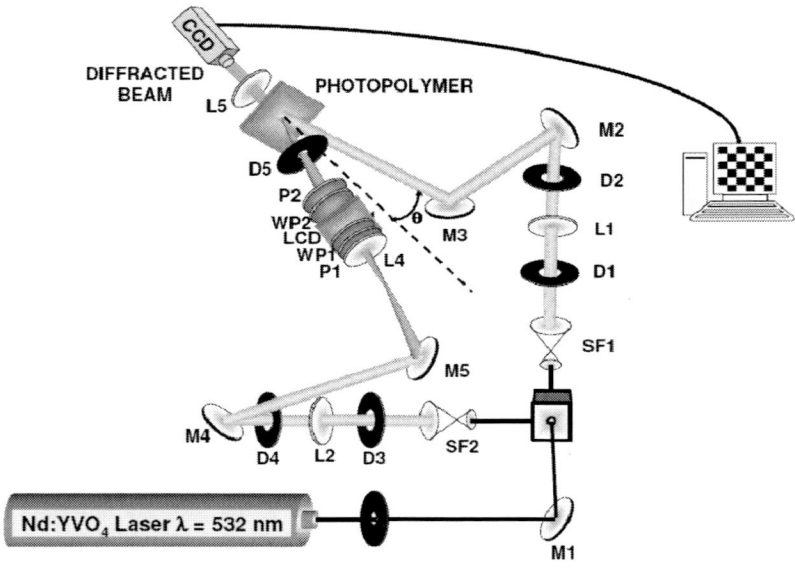

Figure 7. Experimental setup: BS beam splitter, Mi mirror, Li lens, Di, diaphragm, SFi, microscope objective lens and pinhole, SLM spatial light modulator, Pi polarizer, WPi quarter wave plate, CCD charge coupled device.

In the reconstruction stage, once the object has been stored, the hologram is illuminated with the same reference beam used in the recording stage but with a very low intensity in order not to deform the hologram (since the material is sensitive to this wavelength) [3]. Another lens (L5) was placed behind the photopolymer to perform the optical inverse Fourier transform (IFT) of the diffracted beam on the surface of the charge-coupled device (CCD). A computer sent the data pages to the LCD and another computer acquired the images reconstructed by the CCD. This holographic setup will be used to store data pages in the material, using the two modulations described before.

2.4. Bit Error Rate

After one of the objects has been stored in the material, the hologram is reconstructed by illuminating it with the reference beam, and the obtained diffracted beam is imaged onto the CCD. If the holographic reconstruction had been perfect, the obtained images would have had white and black uniform pixels. However, the white and black regions usually have a large number of gray levels, which distort the image. For this reason, it is convenient to measure the Bit Error Rate (BER), which is a parameter that quantifies the image quality. The BER is defined as the probability of having erroneous bits in the image. To calculate the BER [23], first we must represent the probability density of obtaining a certain gray level in the region corresponding to the black and to the white [54,55]. These two probability densities are clearly distinguishable for low BER values, although there is a point at which they intersect. This intersection point of both distributions is called x_c.

Once the probability densities have been obtained, both distributions are fitted to a certain known type probability density. In this study, they are fitted to a Gaussian probability distribution given by:

$$W(x_0, \sigma; x) = \frac{1}{\sqrt{2\pi}\sigma} \exp\left(-\frac{(x-x_0)^2}{2\sigma^2}\right) \qquad (6)$$

where x represents each gray level in the image, x_0 the point at which the Gaussian distribution is centred (the mean) and σ the width of the Gaussian distribution (the standard deviation). The reason why the previous distributions are fitted to a Gaussian equation is that it has been verified that most probability distributions obtained from an image captured by a CCD may be expected to follow this type of distribution.

Once the adjustments for the probability densities of both white and black pixels have been carried out, the BER is calculated as:

$$BER = \frac{1}{2}\left[\int_0^{x_c} W_W(x)dx + \int_{x_c}^{\infty} W_B(x)dx\right] \qquad (7)$$

where W_W and W_B are the adjustments of the probability densities for the white and black pixels respectively, and x_c is the point of intersection of the two probability densities. Using this algorithm, the BER of all the images shall be calculated and discussed in the following sections.

2.5. Binary Intensity Modulation and Hybrid Ternary Modulation for Holographic Data Storage

In this section we are going to multiplex four data pages of different bit sizes in a photopolymer plate with a thickness of 500 μm, an angular separation of 3° and a beam ratio R = 100. Once it is stored, it will rebuild with an intensity I_R=0.3mW/cm^2 by capturing the image obtained with a CCD camera. In previous studies it was found that these were the most suitable parameters to get the best image quality [55]. To store as many holograms as possible in the photopolymer, the exposure is increased gradually for the successive holograms so that the latest holograms have the same diffraction efficiency as the initial ones. When all the holograms are stored, they are reconstructed at the end of the registration process with the reference beam, and the diffracted images are captured with a CCD. The BER is then calculated from these images [23,54,55]. This storage process will be carried out for both the binary modulation in intensity and the HTM.

First, data pages are stored using the binary intensity modulation. Figure 8 depicts with empty triangles the exposure for which the holograms will be stored using this modulation. The first object to be stored has a size of 300x300 bits, and its BER is depicted with full circles in Figure 8. For this object, 58 holograms are achieved with a BER below 0.2. In other studies, it has been shown that BER values below 0.2 provide good image quality. For this reason, in this work we consider that the BER values lower than 0.2 are those that provide the best quality images. The holograms 1 to 50 have been stored with a BER value of 0.02. From hologram 51, the BER values increase but remain below 0.2. Then the object of 400x400 bits is stored, and its BER is depicted with empty circles in Figure 8. In this case, 39 holograms are stored with BER values below 0.2. The next object to store has a size of 500x500 bits and it is depicted with full squares in figure 8. In this case, 42 holograms are stored with a BER below 0.2. Finally, we have multiplexed an object of 800x600 bits, whose BER values are depicted with empty squares. As can be appreciated, 53 holograms have been stored with a BER below 0.2.

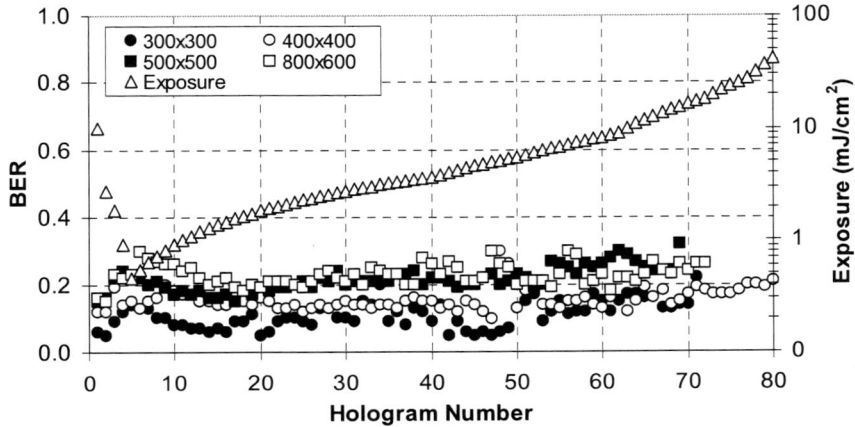

Figure 8. BER of the objects, in a 500 μm thickness material.

Second, the four objects are stored using the HTM to modulate the object beam [56]. The exposure used for storage is depicted with empty triangles in Figure 9. In this same figure, the BER values obtained for each object are also shown.

In this figure, full circles show the BER of holograms stored for the object of 300x300 bits. Notice that 71 holograms with an average BER of 0.11 have been stored. The object of 400x400 bits is depicted with empty circles in Figure 9, for which it has achieved an average BER of 0.16 for 80 multiplexed holograms. Then, the object of 500x500 bits is stored, and the BER values obtained are depicted with full squares in Figure 9. In this case, 68 holograms have been obtained with an average BER of 0.21. Finally, an object of 800x600 bits is multiplexed in the material and the corresponding BER values are depicted with empty circles in Figure 9. In this case, 72 holograms have been multiplexed with an average BER of 0.23.

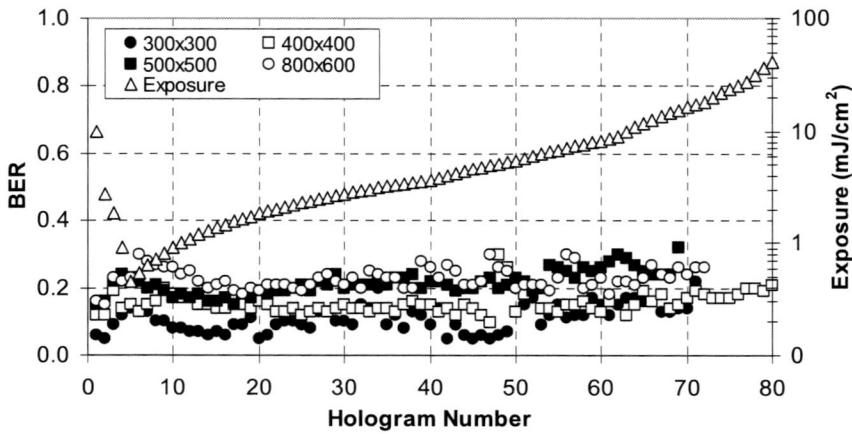

Figure 9. BER and exposure of the objects stored with the HTM configuration in a 500 μm thick material.

Finally, we will compare the results with the thickness of 500 μm for the two modulations.

For binary intensity modulation between 39 and 58 holograms with BER values close to zero have been stored. The HTM has stored between 70 and 80 holograms with BER values lower than 0.2. However, from these results we can conclude that the BER of the images increases and the image quality decreases when the number of bits in the objects increases. When the bit size is larger, the effects of blurring due to the high material thickness were not remarkable. However, when the bit size was reduced, blurring appeared in the image, decreasing its quality.

CONCLUSION

In this chapter, storage capacity of a photopolymer has been analyzed for use as a holographic memory. For this purpose, 90 diffraction gratings have been multiplexed in photopolymer layers of 700 μm thickness. Secondly, we have multiplexed data pages with different pixel sizes by using two types of object beam modulation: binary intensity modulation and hybrid ternary modulation.

The advantage of holographic storage using binary intensity modulation is that it allows image quality with very low BER values regardless of the thickness of the recording material. The disadvantages of such type of modulation are that they do not allow storage of a large number of holograms (maximum 58 holograms with a thickness of 500 µm) and that this type of storage is very sensitive to defects in the recording material.

In the case of the HTM, the main advantage is that one can store a greater number of holograms (80 to 500 µ m thick). Furthermore, such storage is not sensitive to defects in the recording material. However, it has been observed that increasing the thickness of the material gives rise to a blur in the image and increases the BER values depending on the resolution of the object.

REFERENCES

[1] Dhar, L.; Curtis, K.; Fäcke, T. *Nat. Phot.* 2008, vol. 2, 403-405.
[2] Graham-Rowe, D. *Nat. Phot.* 2007, vol. 1, 197-200.
[3] Lu, K.; Saleh, B. E. A. *Opt. Eng.* 1990, vol. 29, 240-246.
[4] Yamauchi, M.; Eiju, T. *Opt. Comm.* 1995, vol. 115, 19-25.
[5] Kim, H.; Lee, Y. H. *Appl. Opt.* 2005, vol. 44, 1642-1649.
[6] Márquez, A.; Iemmi, C.; Moreno, I.; Davis, J. A.; Campos, J.; Yzuel, M. J. *Opt. Eng.* 2001, vol. 40, 2558-2564.
[7] Marquez, A.; Gallego, S.; Mendez, D.; Alvarez, M. L.; Fernandez, E.; Ortuno, M.; Neipp, C.; Belendez, A.; Pascual, I. *Opt. Lett.* 2007, vol. 32, 2511-2513.
[8] Guerrero, R. A. *Opt. Comm.* 2005, vol. 245, 75-83.
[9] Joseph, J.; Waldman, D. A. *Appl. Opt.* 2006, vol. 45, 6374-6380.
[10] Remenyi, J.; Varhegyi, P.; Domjan, L.; Koppa, P.; Lorincz, E. *Appl. Opt.* 2003, vol. 42, 3428-3434.
[11] Renu, J.; Joby, J.; Kehar, S. *Opt. Laser Eng.* 2005, vol. 43, 183-194.
[12] Márquez, A.; Gallego, S.; Mendez, D.; Alvarez, M. L.; Fernández, E.; Ortuño, M.; Neipp, C.; Beléndez, A.; Pascual, I. *Opt. Lett.* 2007, vol. 32, 2511-2513.
[13] Das, B.; Vyas, S.; Joseph, J.; Senthilkumaran, P.; Singh, K. *Opt. Laser Eng.* 2009, vol. 47, 1150-1159.
[14] Das, B.; Joseph, J.; Singh, K. *Opt. Comm.* 2009, vol. 282, 2147-2154.
[15] Domjan, L.; Koppa, P.; Szarvas, G.; Remenyi, J. *Optik*, 2002, vol. 113, 382-390.

[16] Márquez, A.; Gallego, S.; Méndez, D.; Álvarez, M. L.; Fernández, E.; Ortuño, M.; Beléndez, A.; Pascual, I. In Liquid crystals and applications in optics; Glogarova, M.; PalffyMuhoray, P.; Copic, M., eds.; *Proceeding of SPIE*, US, 2007; Vol. 6587, pp 58715-58715.
[17] Jang, J. S.; Shin, D. H. *Opt. Lett.* 2001, vol. 26, 1797-1799.
[18] Ortuño, M.; Gallego, S.; García, C.; Neipp, C.; Beléndez, A.; Pascual, I. *Appl. Phys. B.* 2003, vol. 76, 851-857.
[19] Schnoes, M.; Ihas, B.; Hill, A.; Dhar, L.; Michaels, D.; Setthachayanon, S.; Schomberger, G.; Wilson, W. L. In Practical Holography XVII and Holographic Materials IX; Tung H.Jeong, ed.; *Proceeding of SPIE*, US, 2003; Vol. 5005, pp 29-37.
[20] Mcleod, R. R.; Daiber, A. J.; McDonald, M. E.; Robertson, T. L.; Slagle, T.; Sochava, S. L.; Hesselink, L. *Appl. Opt.* 2005, vol. 44, 3197-3207.
[21] Pu, A.; Psaltis, D. *Appl. Opt.* 1996, vol. 35, 2389-2398.
[22] Pu, A.; Curtis, K.; Psaltis, D. Opt. Eng. 1996, vol. 35, 2824-2829.
[23] Coufal, H.; Psaltis, D.; Sincerbox, G. T. Holographic Data Storage; Springer-Verlag: New Cork, 2000.
[24] El Hafidi, I.; Grzymala, R.; Kiefer, R.; Elouad, L.; Meyrueis, P. *Opt. Laser Technol.* 2005, vol. 37, 503-508.
[25] Curtis, K.; Pu, A.; Psaltis, D. Opt. Lett. 1994, vol. 19, 993-994.
[26] Sherif, H.; Naydenova, I.; Martin, S.; McGinn, C.; Toal, V. J. Opt. A: *Pure Appl. Opt.* 2005, vol. 7, 255-260.
[27] Rakuljic, G. A.; Leyva, V.; Yariv, A. Opt. Lett. 1992, vol. 17, 1471-1473.
[28] Cao, L. C.; Ma, X. S.; He, Q. S.; Long, H.; Wu, M. X.; Jin, G. F. *Opt. Eng.* 2004, vol. 43, 2009-2016.
[29] Bunsen, M.; Okamoto, A.; Takayama, Y. Opt. Comm. 2004, vol. 235, 41-47.
[30] Hariharan, P. Basics of Holography; Cambridge University Press: United Kingdom, 2002.
[31] Hsu, K. Y.; Lin, S. H.; Hsiao, Y. N.; Whang, W. T. *Opt. Eng.* 2003, vol. 42, 1390-1396.
[32] Kim, W. S.; Chang, H. S.; Jeong, Y. C.; Lee, Y. M.; Park, J. K.; Shin, C. W.; Nam, K.; Tak, H. J. *Opt. Comm.* 2005, vol. 249, 65-71.
[33] Barachevskii, V. A. *High Energy Chem*. 2006, vol. 40, 131-141.
[34] Ramos, G.; Álvarez-Herrero, A.; Belenguer, T.; Levy, D.; del Monte, F. In Organic Holographic Materials and Applications; Meerholz, K., ed.; *Proceeding of SPIE*, US, 2003; Vol. 5216, pp 116-126.

[35] Lin, S. H.; Chen, P. L.; Hsiao, Y. N.; Whang, W. T. *Opt. Comm.* 2008, vol. 281, 559-566.
[36] Luo, S. J.; Chen, K. X.; Cao, L. C.; Liu, G. D.; He, Q. S.; Jin, G. F.; Zeng, D. X.; Chen, Y. *Opt. Express*, 2005, vol. 13, 3123-3128.
[37] Banyal, R. K.; Prasad, B. R. *Opt. Comm.* 2007, vol. 274, 300-306.
[38] Hackel, M.; Kador, L.; Kropp, D.; Schmidt, H. W. *Adv. Mater.* 2007, vol. 19, 227.
[39] Ortuño, M.; Fernández, E.; Gallego, S.; Beléndez, A.; Pascual, I. *Opt. Express*, 2007, vol. 15, 12425-12435.
[40] Ortuño, M.; Fernández, E.; Gallego, S.; Márquez, A.; Neipp, C.; Pascual, I.; Beléndez, A. In Practical Holography Xxii: Materials and Applications; Bjelkhagen, H.; Kostuk, R., eds.; *Proceeding of SPIE*, US, 2008; Vol. 6912, pp 91207-91207.
[41] Gallego, S.; Ortuño, M.; García, C.; Neipp, C.; Beléndez, A.; Pascual, I. *J. Mod. Opt.* 2005, vol. 52, 1575-1584.
[42] Mok, F. H.; Burr, G. W.; Psaltis, D. *Opt. Lett.* 1996, vol. 21, 896-898.
[43] Yan, A. Q.; Tao, S. Q.; Wang, D. Y.; Shi, M. Q.; Wu, F. P. In Advances in optical data storage technology; Duanyi Xu; Kees A.Schouhamer Immink; Keiji Shono, eds.; *Proceeding of SPIE*, US, 2005; Vol. 5643, pp 109-117.
[44] Murciano, A.; Blaya, S.; Carretero, L.; Ulibarrena, M.; Fimia, A. *Appl. Phys. B.* 2005, vol. 81, 167-169.
[45] Fernández, E.; García, C.; Pascual, I.; Ortuño, M.; Gallego, S.; Beléndez, A. *Appl. Opt.* 2006, vol. 45, 7661-7666.
[46] Fernández, E.; Ortuño, M.; Gallego, S.; García, C.; Beléndez, A.; Pascual, I. *Appl. Opt.* 2007, vol. 46, 5368-5373.
[47] Fernández, E.; Ortuño, M.; Márquez, A.; Gallego, S.; Pascual, I. In Photon Management Ii; Sheridan, J. T.; Wyrowski, F., eds.; *Proceeding of SPIE*, US, 2006; Vol. 6187, pp U391-U397.
[48] Durán, V.; Lancis, J.; Tajahuerce, E.; Jaroszewicz, Z. J. *Appl. Phys.* 2005, vol. 97, 043101/1-043101/6.
[49] Márquez, A.; Iemmi, C.; Campos, J.; Yzuel, M. J. *Opt. Lett.* 2006, vol. 31, 392-394.
[50] Fernández, E.; Ortuño, M.; Gallego, S.; García, C.; Márquez, A.; Beléndez, A.; Pascual, I. In Practical Holography Xxii: Materials and Applications; Bjelkhagen, H.; Kostuk, R., eds.; *Proceeding of SPIE*, US, 2008; Vol. 6912, pp 91214.
[51] Márquez, A.; Campos, J.; Yzuel, M. J.; Moreno, I.; Davis, J. A.; Iemmi, C. *Opt. Eng.* 2000, vol. 39, 3301-3307.

[52] Soutar, C.; Lu, K. *Opt. Eng.* 1994, vol. 33, 2704-2712.
[53] Davis, J. A.; Allison, D. B.; D'Nelly, K. G.; Wilson, M. L.; Moreno, I. *Opt. Eng.* 1999, vol. 38, 705-709.
[54] Fernández, E.; Ortuño, M.; Gallego, S.; Márquez, A.; García, C.; Beléndez, A.; Pascual, I. *Appl. Opt.* 2008, vol. 47, 4448-4456.
[55] Fernández, E.; Ortuño, M.; Gallego, S.; Márquez, A.; García, C.; Fuentes, R.; Beléndez, A.; Pascual, I. *Optik*, 2010, vol. 121, 151-158.
[56] Fernández, E.; Márquez, A.; Gallego, S.; Fuentes, R.; García, C.; Pascual, I. J. *Lightwave Technol.* 2010, vol. 28, 776-783.

In: Data Collection and Storage
Editor: Julian R. Eiras

ISBN 978-1-61209-689-6
© 2012 Nova Science Publishers, Inc.

Chapter 3

NOVEL METALLIC NANOCLUSTER-BASED STRUCTURES AND SEMICONDUCTOR THIN FILMS FOR INFORMATION STORAGE

H. Khlyap^{1+}, V. Laptev^{2*} and L. Panchenko^{3}

^{1}Distelstr.12, D-67657 Kaiserslautern, Germany
^{2}Russian New University, Radio str. 22,
105005 Moscow, Russian Federation
^{3}Sumy State University, Rimskii-Korsakov-str. 2,
UA-40007 Sumy, Ukraine

ABSTRACT

Investigations of various structures for manufacture of nonvolatile memory cells have been performed for decades. Memory elements based on semiconductor structures (thin film transistors, organic bistable devices, floating gate MOSFETs, etc.) are of special interest. Novel metallic nanocluster-based structures formed on conventional silicon substrates have exhibited unique dark currents at room temperature. The relict radiation and the photonic gas seem to be unique macro-medium

---

[+] Email: hkhlyap@yahoo.com
[*] Dr. V. I. Laptev,
Dr. Sc., Russian New University,
Moscow, Russian Federation
Email: viktor.laptev@yahoo.com

containing information about the first moments of our Universe's life and its future. Chalcogenide semiconductors demonstrated interesting features as attractive media for optical information storage. Experimental results described here show a good perspective for using $Ag_3(Tl_3)SbS_3$ semiconductor thin films fabricated by the pulse laser deposition method for long-time storage of optical information. The structure of the films was identified by X-ray diffraction examination as an amorphous with nanoscale crystalline phase inclusions. The current-voltage investigations were performed at room temperature and under applied bias up to 10 V in both directions and showed a domination of tunneling current. Studies of room-temperature electric field-induced characteristics of the active elements mentioned above are reported in this chapter from the point of view of future application and design of novel, reliable and low-cost memory devices.

INTRODUCTION

How to store information? This age-old question existed since human beings first started to make rock pictures. Now the problems of information storage are solved by novel nanophysics and nanotechnology. Among them high-temperature superconductivity and processes in metallic cluster-based nanostructures (for example, dark currents in metals under room temperature without external electric field [1]) open ways for principally new methods of information storage. One can select the following directions in the field: quantum computing, development of nanotube-based memory devises, and pulse holography. We briefly sketch these directions and then present unique experimental results, which can provide a good base for designing perspective memory and information storage devices.

Quantum computing (QC) has become a very hot topic in the past few years [2]. In contrast to classic computers, QC deals with quantum information processing. In quantum computers, the ones and zeros of classical digital computers are replaced by the quantum state of a two-level system. In short, QC is based on the controlled time evolution of the quantum mechanical system [2].

Classic computers operate with bits; quantum computers operate with quantum bits that have named qubits. Unlike their classic counterparts, which have states of only 0 or 1, qubits can be in a complex linear superposition of both states until they are finally read out. For example, the states of a spin ½ particle can be used for quantum computation [2]. For a qubit, the values of the classic bit (0 and 1) are replaced by the ground state ($|0>$) and the excited ($|1>$) state of a quantum two-level system [2].

While one classic bit of information is stored as either 0 or 1, qubit can be in a weighted superposition of both states [2]. For example, $a|0> + b(|1>)$ can be used to encode information in a qubit. This fact provides massive parallelism of QC due to superposition of states when measured with a readout operator, the qubit appears to collapse to state $|0>$ with probability $|a|^2$, and to state $|1>$ with probability $|b|^2$ [2]. The state of two qubits can be written as a four-dimensional vector $|\psi> = a|00> + b|01> + c|10> + d|11>$, where $a^2 + b^2 + c^2 + d^2 = 1$ [2]. The probability of measuring the amplitude of each state is given by the magnitude of its squared coefficient. In general, the state of n qubits is specified by ($2^{n+1} - 1$) real numbers – an exponentially large amount of information – relative to the number of physical particles required [2]. Most of these states are entangled – to create them requires some kind of interaction between the qubits, and the qubits cannot be treated entirely independently from one another. An entangled state cannot be written simply as a product of the states of individual qubits [2]. To maintain the coherence in the system using the qubits for information processing it seems possible to use the quasi-particle spectrum in superconductors that is characterized by an energy gap [2].

Rapid success in the technology of nano-devices, especially various nanotube-based structures made it possible to design novel memory elements. Information storage in nanotube devices undoubtedly seems to be attractive because the storage node can be scaled down to molecular dimensions and the inherent switching times are estimated to be extremely fast [3].

Effective and cheap information storage in semiconductor memory cells is one of the primary reasons for the success of Si-based information technology in the last decades [4]. Until now, the necessarily increased charge storage density of the capacitor with decreasing cell area of new DRAM generations has been achieved by thinning the dielectric film and enlarging the capacitor area using the third dimension [4]. This 3-D folding has been employed since the 4 Mb generations. As the technology enters the Gb DRAM generations, these solutions are reaching their limits; the thickness of the dielectric film (< 4 nm) because of unacceptable charge losses due to tunneling leakage currents, and the 3-D folding because of the production complexity and, thus, reliability, yield and unacceptable costs. Therefore, for the first time, since the introduction of the DRAM, new dielectric materials with higher effective permittivity compared to that of Si nitride/oxide composites, $\varepsilon_r \approx 7$, must be considered for higher density DRAM generations [4].

Holography, in particular, the pulse holography, is also a very perspective method for optical information storage by using various thin film-based structures as a storage media. To increase the recording velocity and mechanical stability of holographic storage systems, the intensity for the writing process has to be increased to get a short recording time [5]. One possibility is to use pulsed laser systems, which provide both short laser pulses in the range of nanoseconds and large intensities. Additionally, in organic materials present unique effects if illuminated with short laser pulses, and can be used for an efficient recording of holograms [5]. Most interesting is the excitation of small polarons in oxide photorefractive crystals, which provide a two-step recording process [5].

NOVEL METALLIC CLUSTER-BASED STRUCTURES AS A POSSIBLE MEDIUM FOR DATA STORAGE

The unique room-temperature electrical characteristics of the porous metallic nanocluster-based structures were described in [1, 6]. We have analyzed the current-voltage characteristics of Cu-Ag-metallic nanocluster contact stripes deposited on conventional crystalline silicon-based solar cells and we have for the first time presented observations of dark currents in metallic structures. Structural investigations [7] demonstrated that copper particles are smaller than 0.1 µm and smaller than the pore diameter in silver (Figure1).

Figure 1. Electron-beam image of the surface of a silver contact prepared as a stripe geometry element obtained on a wafer after copper deposition.

Further studies of the electric field-induced properties of these structures carried out at room temperature (the experimental setup has been described elsewhere [1, 6, 7]) have shown interesting features. Figure 2 plots a double-logarithmic current-voltage characteristic of the Cu-Ag/Si structure measured at the applied electric field (0-400) V/m.

As shown, both "forward" and 'reverse" currents can be described by the function $I = f(V_a)^m$, where I is the experimental current (registered under the forward or reverse direction of the applied electric field), and V_a is an applied voltage. The exponential factor m changes from 1.7 for the "forward" current at V_a up to 50 mV and then decreases down to ~1.0 as the applied bias increases up to 400 mV; for the "reverse" current the factor m is almost constant (~1.0) in the total range of the external electric field. Thus, these experimental current-voltage characteristics (we have to remember that the investigated structure is a metallic cluster-based quasi-nanowire!) can be described according to the theory [8] as follows: the first section of forward current $I = T_{tun}A_{el}(4\varepsilon/9L^2)(2e/m^*)^{1/2}(V_a)^{3/2}$ (ballistic mode) and the second one as $I = T_{tun}A_{el}(2\varepsilon v_s/L^2)V_a$, and the reverse current is $I = T_{tun}A_{el}(2\varepsilon v_s/L^2)V_a$ (velocity saturation mode). Here T_{tun} is a tunneling transparency coefficient of the potential barrier formed by the ultrathin native oxide films, A_{el} and L are the electrical area and the length of the investigated structure, respectively, ε is the electrical permittivity of the structure, m^* is the effective mass of the charge carriers in the metallic Cu-Ag-nanocluster structure, and v_s is the carrier velocity [8]. These experimental data lead to the conclusion that the charge carriers can be ejected from the pores of the Cu-Ag-nanocluster wire in the potential barrier and drift under applied electric field [9].

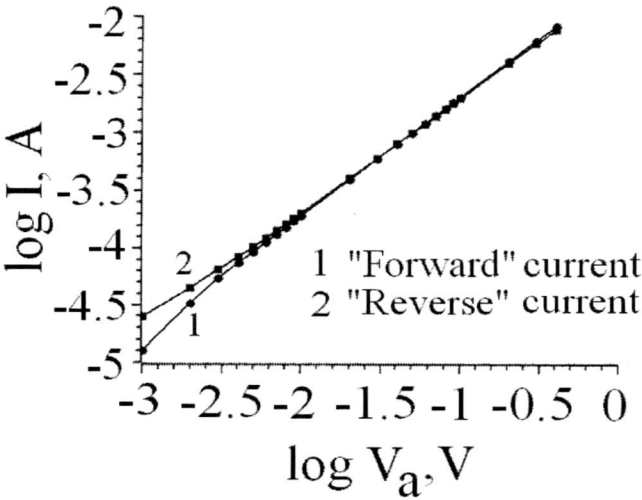

Figure 2. Experimental current-voltage characteristic of the examined structure in double-logarithmic scale (T = 300 K).

Figure 3 plots the change of the resistance observed in the investigated structure at room temperature. Despite the presence of the native oxide films, the absolute values of the resistance are in the range $(12-24) \cdot 10^{-3}$ Ohm. The resistance switching can be attributed to the changes in the potential of the barrier formed immediately after the structure preparation, due to the charge carriers trapping/detrapping in the surface states [10]. These results show a possibility of using the Cu-Ag-nanocluster metallic structures as building blocks for future memory elements.

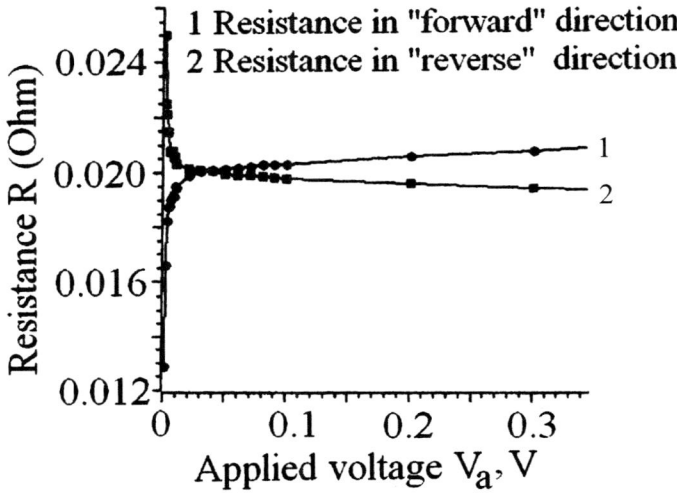

Figure 3. Resistance of the investigated structure as a function of the applied voltage (T = 300 K).

PHOTON CONDENSATE AS AN INFORMATION STORAGE MEDIUM IN THE UNIVERSE

Now we consider the macro-media, which contains very important information about our Universe. Let us remember that the cosmology, thermodynamics, and information theory are closely connected.

The hypothesis about the existence of a photon condensate as a component of the relic radiation was not known until recently. It is based on the assumption of the photon non-zero rest mass [11]. Here we show how the medium consisting of the heat radiation and the photonic condensate may be completely described by the thermodynamic laws.

The entropy S and volume V in the well-known Clapeyron equation [12, 13]

$$dp/dT = S/V \qquad (1)$$

describe the equilibrium of two phases in the case when the pressure of the medium p depends on the medium temperature T only. The pressure of the photon gas is

$$p = \sigma T^4 /3, \qquad (2)$$

where σ is the Stephan-Boltzmann constant. The expressions (1) and (2) completely define the thermodynamic state of the radiation and do not exclude its condensation. However, the photon condensate as a medium containing the information about first moments of our Universe' life and its further destiny has not yet been found. In order to possibly identify this work for the first time we investigate the hypothetic equilibrium between the photon gas and the condensate.

Let us consider the photon gas and condensate as a homogeneous medium in the volume V without phase boundaries. This system will be called "medium", and the parameters of the condensate will be denoted by the corresponding index. The photons and the particles of the condensate have no volume. Then $dV = dV_{cond}$, and the condition of the mechanical equilibrium of the medium $pdV + p_{cond}dV_{cond} = 0$ is reduced to the expression

$$p_{cond} = -p. \qquad (3)$$

The equation (3) describing the positive pressure p of the radiation and the negative pressure p_{cond} of the condensate and the equation (2) mean that

$$p_{cond} = -\sigma T^4/3. \qquad (4)$$

While $dp_{cond} = -4\sigma T^3 dT/3$, the Clapeyron equation for the condensate is written as follows:

$$d(-p_{cond})/dT = S/V,$$

if the entropy of the condensate is assumed to be equal to the entropy of the photon gas, i.e.

$$S_{cond} = S = 4\sigma T^3 V/3. \qquad (5)$$

The expressions (3) - (5) completely define the thermodynamic state of the medium with the equilibrium of positive and negative pressure.

According to the condition (3), the condensate and the radiation transform the energy U into the form of mechanical work. Therefore, $dU_{cond} = -p_{cond}dV$. The pressure does not depend on the volume, and the density of energy $u \equiv U/V$ is

$$u_{cond} = -p_{cond} \tag{6}$$

with a precision up to a constant value. In the medium with equilibrium due to expressions (3) – (6)

$$u_{cond} = \sigma T^4/3. \tag{7}$$

The enthalpy of the condensate presented as a function $H = U + pV$ is equal to zero. The differential of this function $dH = TdS + Vdp$ is also equal to zero. Thus, $dS_{cond} = 0$, $dp_{cond} = 0$, and the participation of the condensate in the energy transformation into the form of heat is excluded.

The stability of thermodynamic media is closely connected with the Gibbs' energy G [12-14]. The value G is negative for the condensate and is equal to $-4\sigma T^3 V/3$. For the photon gas $G = 0$. It means that the photon gas is not stable at the condensation process; at the same time, the medium can reach the thermodynamic equilibrium if the conditions for the gas and condensate presented below are satisfied.

The general condition of the thermodynamic medium stability is that the entropy variations are equal to zero [12-14]. The entropy of the medium is $S + S_{cond}$. The solution of the equations $\delta S + \delta S_{cond} = 0$ and $T\delta S = \delta U + p\delta V$ is as follows:

$$(\delta U + p\delta V)/T + (\delta U_{cond} + p_{cond}\delta V)/T_{cond} = 0. \tag{8}$$

The virtual changes of δU and δV for the gas and condensate are written as

$$\delta U = -\delta U_{cond}, \quad \delta V = \delta V_{cond}$$

because of the constraint equations $U + U_{cond} = \text{const}$, $V = V_{cond} = \text{const}$. Solving them together with the equation (8) we find

$$(1/T_{cond} - 1/T)\,\delta U_{cond} + (p_{cond}/T_{cond} + p/T)\,\delta V = 0.$$

The variations δU_{cond} and δV_{cond} are independent. Thus, the equations

$$T = T_{cond}, \qquad p = -p_{cond} \qquad (9)$$

re conditions of the thermodynamic equilibrium of the medium. However, due to the constraint equation (2) it is enough to indicate the temperature or pressure, or a chemical potential of the photon gas to fix the equilibrium.

Let us assume the medium is cooling under the adiabatic extension according to the equilibrium conditions (9). Suppose the medium departs from the equilibrium. The condensate extension will be continued with the constant value p^* due to the condition $dp_{cond} = 0$. The ratio $(-p^*/p)$ increases with the decrease of the pressure p of the radiation. The domination of the negative pressure p^* arises, and the medium obtains a positive acceleration. At the accelerated extension of the medium the energy density u^* of the condensate is constant, $u^* = -p^*$. At the extension, the medium performs work without energy change: the condensate becomes energy of the radiation.

The relic radiation is an example of the photon gas, which is steadily cooled under adiabatic extension. Supposing the relic condensate exists, we connect the beginning of the accelerated extension of the Universe with fixation of the energy density u^* of the condensate. On the other hand, the positive cosmological acceleration is attributed to the adiabatic medium having the constant energy density 4 GeV/m^3. The nature of this energy is unknown [15-17]. Can the relic condensate be a part of this medium because the cosmological medium and the photon condensate have the same equation of the state $u = -p$?

The relic condensate has the energy density of 4 GeV/m^3 according to the expression (7), when the temperature of the relic radiation is 40 K. If the positive acceleration of the cosmological extension arises at this temperature, the density of the condensate becomes a constant value u^*, and the fraction x of the energy of the relic condensate in the energy of the cosmological medium is equal to 1. If the accelerated extension of the cosmological medium arises at $T^* < 40$ K, then $x = (T^*/40)^4$. According to the Friedman model $T^* = 4.6$ K [18], and the part of the relic condensate can be equal to 0.02% of the cosmological medium.

Therefore, it should be noted that the negative pressure appears in the medium consisting of the particles without volume. The equilibrium of the negative and positive pressure is a main entity of the Clapeyron equation for the photon gas with a condensate. When this equilibrium is broken, the medium begins to extend with acceleration due to the domination of the negative pressure. The moment of the Universe development at zero acceleration of the cosmological extension is known. We hope that the modeling of the medium containing the photon gas and condensate enables us to study other features, find unknown relations in the development of the Universe taking place with and without acceleration, and to discover novel aspects of the information hidden in the Universe.

CHALCOGENIDE SEMICONDUCTOR THIN FILMS FOR OPTICAL INFORMATION STORAGE

Now we go back to the perspective of nanostructured objects for information storage. Various thin films prepared by different technologies demonstrated interesting features suitable for solving the problem of the stable optical information storage [5, 19-20]. Among these methods, the pulse laser deposition (PLD) technique is one of the most important tools [5, 19]. Further, we report experimental data on investigations of nanostructured Ag-containing chalcogenide semiconductor thin films.

Ag-containing single crystals were used as targets for the PLD of AgSbS films. Glass and alkali halide single crystals were used as substrates. The deposition process was carried out under vacuum level 10^{-3} Pa; the temperature of substrates was 300 and 400 K. The thicknesses of the films varied from 20 to 400 nm. Nd:YAG laser under Q-switched conditions with target surface power density of 10^8 to 10^9 Wcm^{-2} and average pulse duration of about 1 ns served as a principal part of the experimental setup. To obtain the layers with stoichiometry closed to the initial single crystalline targets, the following technological conditions are applied: pulse frequency repetition f = 25 Hz, single pulse energy w = 0.01 J/pulse, the substrate temperature T_s = 400 K and pulse repetition frequency f = 100 Hz, single pulse energy w = 0.003 J/pulse for the substrate temperature T_s = 300 K [19-20]. The typical micrographs of the films prepared on dielectric substrates are presented in Figure 4.

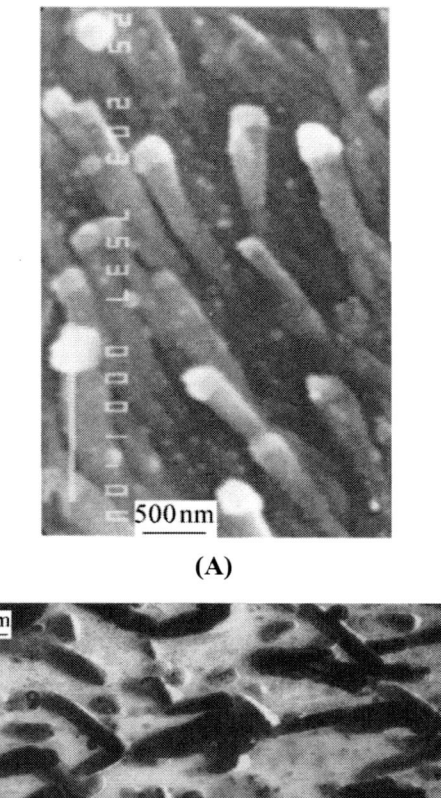

Figure 4. Typical electron microscopic images of Ag_3SbS_3 films grown by the pulse laser deposition technology: a) glass substrate $T_s = 300$ K, $f = 50$ Hz, $w = 0.01$ J/pulse, thickness of the layer is 150 nm, characteristic size of the structural element (column) is estimated to be about 700 nm; b) the same film deposited on KCl substrate at the substrate temperature $T_s = 400$ K, $f = 100$ Hz, $w = 0.01$ J/pulse.

As shown, the films have a strongly inhomogeneous structure. The surface relief sufficiently depends on technological conditions used under the layers' deposition. The porous (columnar-like) structure is obtained at room temperature on glass substrates with intermediate laser pulse repetition frequency f = 50 Hz. Increasing the pulse repetition frequency to 100 Hz enables preparation of films on (001)-oriented KCl wafers with a network-like structure (Figure 4b); we should note that the energy density of the laser pulse is the same in both cases. Detailed morphological examinations of the films [20] showed the dominant amorphous phase with nanocrystalline nuclei. Due to these structural features, the pulse laser deposited Ag_3SbS_3 films seem to attract extensive attention as objects for various memory applications. Note that the electrical properties of these films have rarely been investigated until recently.

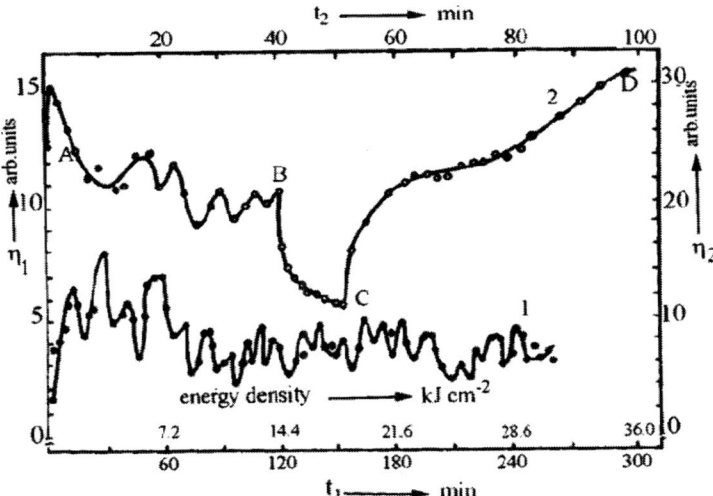

Figure 5. Results of holographic investigations of the pyrargirite films deposited under following technological conditions: T_s = 300 K, f = 100 Hz, d = 100 nm (1) and T_s = 300 K, f = 25 Hz, d = 200 nm (2). Curve AB denotes writing, curve BC represents continuous reading, and curve CD shows rewriting. A diffraction grid with the period L = 450 nm served as an object for write–read process [20].

In order to examine suitability of the prepared layers for optical information storage holograms were written by using two light sources: He-Ne laser with wavelength λ = 633 nm and He-Cd laser with wavelength λ = 442 nm (both devices operated under continuous wave mode). Energy power for writing was estimated to be about $3 W/cm^2$; for reading, this value was equal to 1.5 W/cm^2. The exposition time has varied from 30 min up to 15 h. The dependence of diffraction efficiency η on the energy exposition H_e has been investigated (Figure 5) [20]. Our experiments showed for the first time an oscillating character of time dependence of the diffraction efficiency η for holograms written on thin Ag-containing films. The time function indicates the stability of the films as a medium under different cycles of the write–read process. Time stability of these records was studied after storage of the films for 2-3 years under normal atmospheric conditions. Examination of repeated reading showed no significant changes [20].

Room-temperature electrical properties of Ag-containing films are of particular interest, while the metal-semiconductor structures based on these layers may eject-accumulate charges. Four sets of samples [20] of 3 mm^2 area with *In*-contact pads were chosen for measurements of current–voltage characteristics without any predefined polarity of applied voltage and investigation of the layer resistance and dependence upon growth conditions. Under experiment, the following technological parameters have been varied: substrate temperature T_s, time of deposition t_{growth}, pulse repetition frequency f and type of substrate. The applied electric field F_a did not exceed 3 kV/m in order to prevent the films heating at the electrical measurements. Experimental current–voltage dependencies are shown in Figure 6. They can be qualitatively described by a function $I_{exper} \sim A^*T^2\exp(-e\varphi_B/k_BT)\exp[(eV_a/k_BT) - 1]$, where A^* is the Richardson constant, k_B is the Boltzmann constant, φ_B is the height of the barrier between the grown semiconductor film with a native oxide forming immediately after the finishing deposition and the metal contact, V_a is the applied voltage (relates to the applied electric field as $V_a = F_ad$, where d is the distance between two metal contacts deposited on the film) [8].

As seen, the experimental I-V functions are slightly asymmetrical in both directions of the applied voltage. These data indicate domination of direct tunneling currents typical for semiconductor structures with ultrathin native (thermal) oxide [8, 20]. The transport of the charge carriers flowing through the samples has no dependence on the technological conditions of their preparation. Investigations of the layers' resistance R showed that the films deposited on single crystal KCl substrates (function 1 in Figure 6) have the highest values of R (up to 2×10^9 Ohm), and the films grown on glass substrates are characterized by the smallest resistances (no more than $(4-7)\times10^7$ Ohm). This difference may be explained by Ag excess in phase composition [20]. On the other hand, availability of nanocrystalline phases [20] can enhance the carriers' injection and accumulation in the contact regions prepared on the sample [20, 21].

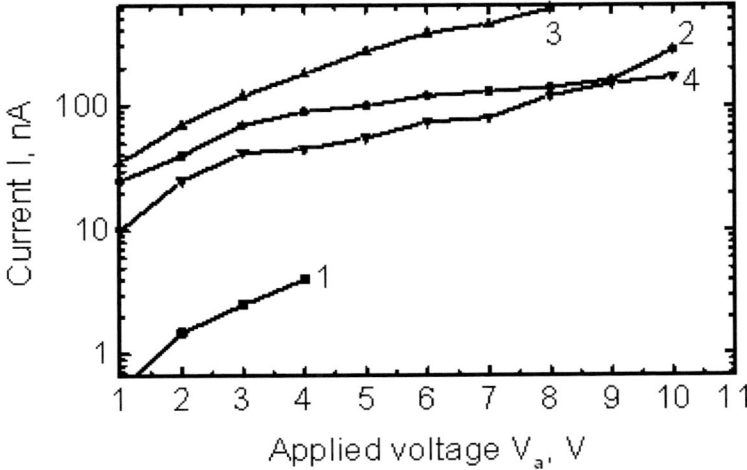

Figure 6. Room temperature current–voltage characteristics (IVC) of the investigated samples without any predefined polarity of the applied voltage. 1: single crystal KCl substrate, $T_s = 400$ K, $f = 25$ Hz, $t_{growth} = 600$ s; 2: glass substrate, $T_s = 300$ K, $f = 25$ Hz, $t_{growth} = 600$ s; 3: single crystal KCl substrate, $T_s = 300$ K, $f = 50$ Hz, $t_{growth} = 900$ s; 4: single crystal KCl substrate, $T_s = 400$ K, $f = 25$ Hz, $t_{growth} = 900$ s.

CONCLUSION

The experimental and theoretical results presented in this communication demonstrate for the first time unique structures and calculations, which can improve our understanding of information storage media. Novel Cu-Ag-nanoclustered porous metallic wires manufactured on conventional silicon wafers show room-temperature space-charge limited currents and resistance switch at extremely low applied voltages.

Theoretical calculations illustrate the discovery of unknown properties of the relic radiation as macro-medium stored information about our Universe; in particular, the following features seem to be of special interest:

i) beginning of the galaxies formation and effects arisen at the same time;
ii) distorting equilibrium between condensate and relic radiation can possibly be observed on objects with red shift 13.2 or lesser.

Nanostructured Ag-containing chalcogenide semiconductor thin films having both porous and network-like structure showed their applicability for long-time optical information storage; besides that, the room-temperature electric field-induced characteristics of the metal-semiconductor active elements based on these films pointed out the possibility of charge ejection-accumulation.

REFERENCES

[1] Laptev, V.; Khlyap, H. *Doklady Physical Chemistry*, 2009, vol. 424(2), 40–42.

[2] Ustinov, A. Quantum computing using superconductors. In: Waser R., editor. Nanoelectronics and Information Technology. Weinheim: WILEY-VCH Verlag GmbH & Co. KGa A; 2005; 995 pp. *See also*: Sun, G. *et al.* Tunable quantum beam splitters for coherent manipulation of a solid-state tripartite qubit system. *Nat. Commun.* 1:51 doi: 10.1038 / ncomms1050 (2010).

[3] Appenzeller, J.; Joselevich, E.; Hönlein, W. Carbon nanotubes for data processing. In: Waser R., editor. Nanoelectronics and Information Technology. Weinheim: WILEY-VCH Verlag GmbH & Co. KGa A; 2005; 995 pp.

[4] Schroeder, H.; Kingon A. High-permettivity materials for DRAMs. In: Waser R., editor. Nanoelectronics and Information Technology. Weinheim: WILEY-VCH Verlag GmbH & Co. KGa A; 2005; 995 pp.

[5] Imlau, M.; Bieringer, T.; Odoulov, S.G.; Woike, T. Holographic data storage. In: Waser R., editor. Nanoelectronics and Information Technology. Weinheim: WILEY-VCH Verlag GmbH & Co. KGa A; 2005; 995 pp.

[6] Laptev, V.I.; Khlyap, H. High-effective solar energy conversion: Thermodynamics, crystallography and clusters. In: Carson J.A., editor. Solar Cell Research Progress. New York: Nova Science Publishers, Inc.; 2008; 329 pp.

[7] Kozar', V.; Karapuzova, N.A.; Laptev, G.V.; Laptev, V.I.; Khlyap, G.M.; Demicheva, O.V.; Tomishko, A.G.; Alekseev, A.M. *Nanotechnologies in Russia*, 2010, vol. 5, pp. 549–553.

[8] Sze, S.M.; Ng, Kwok K. Physics of Semiconductor Devices. New York: Wiley-Interscience Inc., 2007; 815 pp.

[9] Chen, I.S.; Bang, W.H.; Park, Y.-J.; Ryan, E.T.; King, S.; Kim, C.-U. *Appl Phys Lett*. 2010, vol.96, pp.091903-1-091903-3.
[10] Shang, D.S.; Shi, L.; Sun, J.R.; Shen, B.G.; Zhuge, F.; Li, R.W.; Zhao, Y.G. *Appl Phys Lett*. 2010, vol.96, pp. 072103-1-072103-3.
[11] Kuz'min V.A.; Shaposhnikov M.E. *JETP Letters*, 1978, vol.27, pp.628-631.
[12] Kondepudi, D.; Prigogine, I. Modern Thermodynamics: From Heat Engines to Dissipative Structure. New York: Wiley, 1998; 508 pp.
[13] Bazarov, I.P. Thermodynamics. Oxford: Pergamon Press, 1964; 287 pp.
[14] Muenster, A. Classical Thermodynamics. New York: Wiley, 1970; 692 pp.
[15] [15] Chernin, A.D. Phys. Usp. 2008, vol.51, pp.253-282.
[16] [16] Lukash, V.N.; Rubakov, V.A. Phys. Usp. 2008, vol.51, pp. 283-289.
[17] Greene, B. The Fabric of the Cosmos. Space, Time, and Texture with Reality. New York: Alfred A. Knopf, 2004; 569 pp.
[18] Chernin, A.D. Phys. Usp. 2001, vol.44, pp.1099-1118.
[19] Khlyap, H. (2009). Physics and Technology of Semiconductor Thin Film-Based Active Elements and Devices (e-book). Bentham Science Publishers 2009, eISBN 978-1-60805-021-5.www.bentham.org/ebooks
[20] Panchenko, L.; Khlyap, H.; Laptev, V. *Appl. Surf. Science*, 2009, vol. 255, pp. 5256-5259.
[21] Cho, B.; Song, S.; Ji,Y.; and Lee, T. *Appl Phys Lett*. 2010, vol.97, pp. 063305-1-063305-3.

In: Data Collection and Storage
Editor: Julian R. Eiras

ISBN 978-1-61209-689-6
© 2012 Nova Science Publishers, Inc.

Chapter 4

THE INFLUENCE OF BIAS AGAINST TARGET CULTURE ON MOTIVATION OF YOUNG LEARNERS TO LEARN ENGLISH: SOME THOUGHTS ON DATA COLLECTION

Eda Üstünel[1] *and Seyran Öztürk*[2]

[1] Muğla University
Faculty of Education, Department of English Language Teacher Training, Turkey

[2] Muğla University
Faculty of Social Sciences, MA Candidate on English Language Teacher Training
Turkey

ABSTRACT

Up until the introduction of communicative language teaching, language learning was seen as mastering the structures and vocabulary of the target language, but ignored the other factors that are indispensable parts of real communication. Following this point it is impossible to talk about target culture from a monocultural perspective. Culture is not static or homogeneous. Therefore teachers of English may

---

[1] Email: eda.ustunel@gmail.com
[2] Email: ozturkseyran@gmail.com

seek ways of opening new windows for their students by making them aware that other cultures exist all of which bring variety to our world. As English does not represent a singular culture due to its current function, or widespread usage all over the world, its cultural aspect cannot be taught like the other components of the language. The main purpose of this chapter is to identify the influence of bias against target culture on the motivation of young learners to learn English.

The data for this chapter has been collected from students of the 4th and 7th grades at Selimiye Primary School, Milas, Turkey. The research has been carried out with four classes with two classes from the 4th grade and two from the 7th. Questionnaires, interviews and field notes taken by the researchers during observation of the lessons are used to collect the data.

All students are given an attitude scale. With this pre-test, it is aimed to explore the students' attitudes towards other cultures. After the implementation of the pre-test, one class from the 4th grade and one from the 7th are given culturally-focused lessons for one month, enriched with role-play and drama activities. Throughout the implementation, field notes are taken by the researchers and interviews are conducted before and after the activities. After this implementation, a post-test is administered to all participated classes.

INTRODUCTION

For years, many theories have been put forward to explain how people acquire their first language. It has been accepted that there is a critical age period in first language acquisition which is the ideal time for acquiring the language properly. However, for second language acquisition, it is still debatable whether there is such a period or not, although, it is generally accepted the earlier the better. With the developments in the areas of politics, economics and technology, today's world is shrinking, and so people are able to be in contact with other countries and in order to do this, they need a medium language which is the most widely accepted and today, that is English. For these reasons, teaching English in Turkey was changed during the educational reforms of 1997-1998 to start at the 4th grade.

Up until now, various approaches and methods have been introduced to teach and learn a second language. There has been a continuum starting with the Grammar Translation Method and ending with Communicative Language Teaching. The Grammar Translation Method is the most traditional for second language teaching including memorisation of the formulae of the language structures and long vocabulary lists: with the written language seen as superior to the spoken language. Much has since changed, step by step, from the Grammar Translation Method to Communicative Language Teaching. With the introduction of Communicative Language Teaching, all four skills gained importance. It has been understood that to know a language, by just mastering its structures and vocabulary simply wasn't enough.

Hymes (1972) introduced the term "communicative competence", encompassing all types of language knowledge that are employed to interact successfully and effectively. Canale and Swain (1980) defined four components of communicative competence. The first one is grammatical competence: knowledge of lexical morphological, syntactical and phonological features of language, providing the linguistic basis for the rules of usage which normally result in accuracy of performance. The second one is strategic competence that includes communication strategies which we may call into action to compensate for communication break-downs due to performance variables or insufficient competence. The third one is called discourse competence, and includes the ability to deal with the extended use of language in context with keeping the cohesion and coherence of the communication. The last one is sociolinguistic competence which deals with the social rules of language use. Using the appropriate language according to such factors as the role of the participants in a given interaction, their social status, the information they share, and the function of the interaction are important (Alptekin, 2002, pp. 57-58). As teachers try to make communicatively competent learners, they should pay attention to all the components; but, sociolinguistic competence is more abstract than the others for both learners and teachers as it requires experiencing rather than just learning.

For sociolinguistic competence, we need to make a distinction between *"cultural knowledge"* and *"cultural awareness."* Tomlinson and Masuhara (2004) defined cultural knowledge as being "external, static, stereotypical and reduced; being knowledge passed on to a learner from someone else, rather than arising from the learner's own experience. It may include broad generalisations often based on a narrow selection of evidence. Therefore, it can be misleading." Whereas cultural awareness is "emphasises not information about a culture but skills in exploring, observing and understanding difference and sameness, and perhaps most centrally, suspension of judgement, i.e. not being instantly critical of other people's apparently deviant behaviour" (as cited in Broady, 2004, pp. 68-69).

Therefore, as teachers, we should promote our students' cultural awareness. While teachers are raising their students' cultural awareness they should distinguish between the three distinct views put forward by Chambers (2004). The first one is monocultural perspective which refers to target culture as homogeneous, static and monolingual by neglecting the diversity of the cultures. Secondly, multicultural perspective compensates for the one dimensional bias of the monocultural perspective but doesn't fully recognise the dynamic features of the cultures. The last perspective is the intercultural one taking both the dynamic process of change and the diversity of the cultures into account (as cited in Rantz & Horan, 2005).

Intercultural awareness "emphasises that cultures can only be defined in relation to each other. It implies both a 'window' on the culture/cultures of the target countries and a 'mirror' where we discover ourselves in the process of discovering the other culture." Also it implies a shift from *'ethnocentrism'* to *'ethnorelativism'* which is the ability to decentre, to see things from someone else's perspective, to develop 'empathy' as well as an awareness of the intercultural process of change of both individuals and societies arising out of the dynamics of encounters between them (Rantz & Horan, 2005, pp. 210-211). Rantz and Horan (2005) explain 'intercultural communicative competence', or 'intercultural competence' in short as a combination of 'intercultural awareness' with 'communicative competence' (p. 211).

While developing intercultural awareness at the primary level, we should develop activities that trigger the child's natural curiosity about other cultures, on learning about culture process make the child active, get the child to have not only knowledge but the critical thinking ability about the target culture/s as well as his/her own culture and consider the social and emotional responses of the child in dealing with culture (Rantz & Horan, 2005).

The main purpose of this chapter is to identify the influence of bias against target culture on the motivation of young learners to learn English. Until the introduction of communicative language teaching, language learning was seen as mastering the structures and vocabulary of the target language, but ignored the other factors that are indispensable parts of real communication. Alptekin (2002) argues that "Communicative competence, with its standardised native speaker norms, fails to reflect the lingua franca status of English" (p. 60). He explains that "Given the lingua franca status of English, it is clear that much of the world needs and uses English for instrumental reasons such as professional contacts, academic studies, and commercial pursuits. In this context, much communication in English involves (and will increasingly involve) non-native speaker/non-native speaker interactions" (p. 61). Following this point it is impossible to talk about target culture from a monocultural perspective. Culture is not static or homogeneous. Therefore teachers of English may seek ways of opening new windows for their students by making them aware that other cultures exist all of which bring variety to our world. As English does not represent a singular culture due to its current function, or widespread usage all over the world, its cultural aspect cannot be taught like the other components of the language.

In Turkey, most teachers neglect the communicative function of English and teach it just to make the students pass such exams as SBS, ÜDS etc. From our experience, this kind of teaching makes students biased against both English and different cultures apart from theirs. The ways of coping with such kinds of bias and how to make the students gain an insight towards other cultures are two topics that are covered by this research.

DATA COLLECTION PROCEDURE

Before undertaking any research, there are many things we should consider such as deciding on the field, topic, and research question and etc of our chapter. After deciding on the field, topic our research question, we should adopt the appropriate research methods and methodology for our chapter. Cohen, Manion and Morisson (2007) make it clear that by the term methods, it is meant that the range of approaches used in educational research to collect data to be utilised as a basis for inference and interpretation, for explanation and prediction, whereas methodology helps us to understand the process of the research rather than the products of it.

Hatch and Lazaraton (1991, p. 4) highlight that "There is never a 'one and only one' way to carry out a project" (as cited in Dörnyei 2007, p. 307). Dörnyei (2007) and make some suggestions which will help us decide on the appropriate way. Firstly he draws attention to the relationship between the research question and the topic and suggests us to choose the method that will enlighten our way to the answer of our research question. He also explains the term exploratory purpose which arises when we have little knowledge about the target problem as studying insufficiently or inadequate resources in that field. In such a condition, it is necessary to make explorations to get the general picture of the problem. Thirdly, he claims that there can be an existing research tradition in the area and gives example from his own PhD studies on language learning motivation in which quantitative methods are generally adopted. Besides these, as researchers, we may decide our methods by considering our audience to achieve advancement in our environment however, Todd et al. (2004) call this 'illegitimate motives' (as cited in Dörnyei, 2007). Dörnyei also suggests considering practical factors such as supervisor, available support, resources and sample while adopting the method. Lastly, personal style, training and experience with an approach will affect our choice.

For example, a researcher may choose quantitative method for his research in that he believes he is better at it rather than the qualitative one or like the argument in SLA 'nature or nurture', there is such a debate in scientific research area; our training can be effective on our choice rather than our personal characteristics. All of those don't imply opting for only quantitative methods or only qualitative methods in our research, as we can also make use of a mixture of them. But before mentioning the mixture, it is necessary to make a distinction between the quantitative and qualitative methods. Reichardt and Cook (1979) exhibit the divergences between them. Qualitative research is concerned with understanding human behaviour from the researcher's perspective, process-oriented, discovery-oriented, exploratory, inductive, valid, ungeneralisable, naturalistic and uncontrolled observation. However, quantitative research investigates facts of social phenomena without the individuals' traces, is product-oriented, justification-oriented, confirmatory, deductive, reliable, generalisable, obtrusive and controlled measurement (as cited in Nunan, 2004). These two methods can be used in a supportive way to reinforce the research, called triangulation. Qualitative and quantitative methods applied together can make our research more valid or each can be complementary to the other. Each method, of course, has some weaknesses, but by using them together, the strengths of one can compensate for another's weaknesses. Also as Dörnyei (2007) demonstrates, by using them together we can make our work more acceptable to larger audiences, but he warns us against the danger of lacking methodological proficiency by using both, and he suggests cooperation with researchers proficient at the qualitative methods to make up for his own deficiencies.

There are many examples of research that have been carried out using mixed methodologies. An example from Turkey is the MA thesis of İnan (2006), whose title is 'An Investigation into the Effects of Using Games, Drama, and Music as Edutainment Activities on Teaching Vocabulary to Young Learners':

The data of the study were collected via both qualitative and quantitative research methodologies. As quantitative methods, pre-tests, post-tests and memory tests which were given before and after each application were used and the questionnaire which was administered to 750 students and 16 teachers in 16 state primary schools in the city centre and the vicinity of Çanakkale was qualitative. Quantitative methods were used to show the differences between the achievements of the students before and after the application and qualitative methods were used to indicate the attitudes of both the teacher and the students towards the edutainment activities and the frequency of those activities' application (p. i).

Throughout this research both quantitative and qualitative methods are used. Our purpose for using a mixed method is to validate the findings that we will get from quantitative analysis alone. We work with young learners, whose personal view of the world has not reached a certain level of maturity, so they can be directly affected by their peers; i.e., they can be ashamed of advocating a different view and behave in the same way with their peers. For the quantitative method, questionnaires are employed. For the qualitative methods, interviews with students chosen from the sampling group are carried out. In addition, field notes are taken during the implementation of the activities, in order to deepen our understanding and validate the results of the before/after questionnaires administered for the culturally-focused lessons (enriched with role-play and drama activities during the month).

TOOLS FOR DATA COLLECTION

Questionnaires

Questionnaires are widely used to collect data for scientific research. They supply the researcher with a wide range of information in a relatively short time; can even be administered without the presence of the researcher. In this chapter, Likert scales will measure the young learners' attitudes towards the target culture in order to gain a more thorough picture of their attitudes. That is to say, attitudes cannot be so precise as to just mark them as 'like' or 'dislike' etc. Cohen, Manion and Morisson (2007) explain that Likert scales supply a wider range of responses to a question or statement. During the construction of the questionnaires, work can be done in collaboration with a researcher who is proficient in this field.

Interviews

Interviews are one of the data collection tools most frequently used in qualitative research. Yıldırım and Şimşek (2008) put forward that as a first impression, interviews can be thought of as a simple data collection method as they only require basic skills such as listening and speaking that we use in our daily lives, but that is not the case. In a proficient interview mistakes such as prejudices, not listening efficiently etc. that frequently take place during our daily communication, will not occur, rather it is a controlled and disciplined process. There are three types of interviews; unstructured, semi-structured and structured interview. Nunan (2004) explains that responses of the interviewee direct the unstructured interviews whereas, in a semi-structured interview the general route of the interview is decided by the interviewer but the topics guide the interview rather than the predetermined list of questions. On the other hand, the course of the interview is totally predetermined by the interviewer in a structured interview; where there are predetermined questions applied in a certain order. In this chapter, semi-structured interview is used. Here are the reasons for this choice; if the unstructured interview were to be used, we cannot achieve what we have intended as it will be conducted with young learners and due to their limited attention span and generally being self-centred, the interview may end up with different data included within their responses, such as their holiday memories as a family, rather than their own experiences with foreigners. If a structured interview is used, it could create anxiety; as they can feel shy and can't share their opinions freely or openly. It should be kept in mind that young learners need a relaxed atmosphere in which to learn and share better. Therefore, a semi-structured interview has been decided upon, as it will create a relaxed conversational atmosphere, without deviating from the purpose of the interview, thanks to the efficient guidance and direction of the interviewer.

Interviews are carried out after the pre-test so as to support the results of the questionnaire and interviews are applied again after post-test, in order to validate both the field notes taken during the application of the activities and the results of the questionnaire.

Field Notes

Field notes are used frequently during the observation process. Yıldırım and Şimşek (2008) put forward that the researcher tries to take notes by making use of the abbreviations and symbols he developed before the observation. It is impossible to take long and detailed notes during the observation, otherwise ongoing events can probably be missed. Thus, the researcher should balance note taking and observation, he can note short tips to be completed in detail after the observation.

For observation, video cameras and recorders can also be used. They can be better than the field notes as they are permanent records and can be viewed several times, but these techniques can also destroy the spontaneity of the chapter. If we consider we are working with young learners and their limited attention span these can be more risky. For these reasons, field notes are preferred primarily, but video recording can also be tried in this research.

RESEARCH DESIGN

Firstly, a pre-test, which is constructed for measuring their attitudes towards the target culture, is administered with two classes of the 4th grade students and two from the 7th. With this pre test, it is intended to measure whether or not they have any bias against other cultures, and if any, does it change according to variables such as age, gender, and experience with other cultures? In addition, semi-structured interviews are to be administered to verify the results of the questionnaire.

After getting a general idea about the students' attitudes towards other cultures via pre-test, culturally-focused lessons will be applied for one month, enriched with role-play and drama activities. The reason for choosing drama and role-playing activities is that Altay (2005) suggests many ways to develop cultural awareness in the classroom; but for young learners role-play works well, in that they allow young learners to burn off their energy and as they are still at the concrete operational stage we can raise their cultural awareness more easily in this way. Role-play activities provide an opportunity to be emotionally involved in cross-cultural learning and to reflect upon cultural differences. The students can examine their perceptions and treat other cultures with empathy (Kodotchigova, 2002). Zalta (2006) puts forward that dramatising makes children actively involved in a text. This personalisation makes language more meaningful and memorable than traditional ways such as drilling or mechanical repetition.

Zalta (2006) also adds that using drama and role-playing activities with young learners has some certain advantages while teaching language to them:

- Children are encouraged to speak and get the chance to communicate even with limited knowledge by making use of non-verbal communication.
- It creates a relaxing atmosphere.
- Acting in a role-playing activity rather than reading the same dialogue is different in that it involves children through their bodies, minds, emotions, language and social interaction.
- Drama activities are fun and motivating for children.
- It creates collaborative environment in that mostly they have to work with their friends while acting out.
- Young learners don't pay attention to the bits of the language so drama activities are good ways of contextualising the language. (pp. 24-26)

The aim of this chapter is not to teach a specific culture but to make the students gain cultural awareness by making them develop empathy and gain insight into other cultures, so drama activities are thought to work well for this aim. During this implementation process, field notes are taken, and if possible the lessons will be recorded via a camera or tape-recorder.

Lastly, a post-test is carried out in order to demonstrate the differences, if any, that have occurred between the students who have participated in the role-play and drama activities, and those who have not.

A similar study called the Durham Project was carried out by Byram et al. (1991). Their purpose was to discover the effects of teaching French on students' attitudes towards French people and culture. They based their research on a case study, lasting for eight months; also they made use of interviews, and questionnaires. They explain their data collection procedure at three stages:

1) the statistical analysis of the associations between the dependent variable of level of ethnocentricity in respect of French people and the independent variables of exposure to French teaching and other factors

2) qualitative analysis of attitudes towards French people expressed in interviews by pupils in the three different levels of ethnocentricity rating: this also serves to validate the measure of ethnocentricity;
3) qualitative analysis of the specific contribution of language teaching to pupils' knowledge and attitudes, first through the analysis of observations and second through analysis of pupils' accounts in the interviews (p. 106).

They also searched for the effects of gender on their attitudes and found that no matter what their ages, girls have more positive attitudes towards French people than boys. Boys perceived Americans positively out of the three groups, French, German and American. When the age factor is considered, for girls and boys, the younger they are the more negative their attitudes towards the Germans were, Byram et al. point out the reason for this as- having the same linguistic background with the Americans.

With the Durham Project, experience with the target culture was also investigated. The results showed differences from student to student. It is not easy to make a generalisation that people of a certain nation are good or bad. Some of the students that participated the Durham Project said that French people are nice and kind, on the other hand, some said they were rude and not sociable.

CONCLUSION

As a concluding remark, with this chapter it is hoped to shed some light on the endless road of teaching and learning a foreign language. While teaching English or another language, its cultural aspect has still been ignored, at least this is the case in Turkey. Like all around the world, in Turkey, most teachers talk about using English communicatively and everybody complains about not being able to teach and learn English communicatively even after long years in education. Within our teaching careers, this is what we have frequently heard, but we couldn't logically explain the reasons for this failure. Throughout our teaching experience, we observed that most of our students have been biased against other cultures and they continuously question them. All of these issues are what led us to, or triggered the writing of this chapter.

REFERENCES

Alptekin, C. (2002). Towards intercultural communicative competence in ELT. *ELT Journal, 56(1), pp. 57-64.* Retrieved June 22, 2010. http://web.ebscohost.com/ehost/pdfviewer/pdfviewer?vid=2&hid=110&sid=f2ed81be-094f-41f0-91f0-2f1cdefebd63%40sessionmgr114

Altay, F. (2005). Developing cultural awareness. *Journal of language and linguistic studies, 1(2).* Retrieved May 15, 2010. http://www.jlls.org/Issues/Volume1/No.2/firataltay.pdf

Broady, E. (2004). Sameness and difference: The challenge of culture in language teaching. *Language learning journal,* 29, 68-72. Retrieved June 5, 2010. http://www.ittmfl.org.uk/modules/teaching/1g/paper1g4.pdf

Byram, M., Esarte-Sarries, V., Taylor, S., & Allatt, P. (1991). Young people's perceptions of other cultures: The role of foreign language teaching. In D. Buttjes, & M. Byram (Eds.), *Mediating languages and cultures: Towards an intercultural theory of foreign language education* (pp. 103-119). Philadelphia, USA: Multilingual Matters Series.

Canale, M. & Swain, M. (1980). Theoretical bases of communicative approaches to second language teaching and testing. *Applied linguistics* 1, 1-47.

Cohen, L., Manion, L., & Morisson K. (2007). *Research methods in education* (6th ed.). Routledge.

Dörnyei, Z. (2007). *Research methods in applied linguistics.* USA: Oxford University Press.

Hymes, D. (1972). On communicative competence. In J. B. Pride, & J. Holmes (Eds.), *Sociolinguistics* (pp. 269-293). Harmondsworth: Penguin.

İnan, S. (2006). An investigation into the effects of using games, drama, and music as edutainment activities on teaching vocabulary to young learners. (Master's dissertation, Çanakkale Onsekiz Mart University, 2006). Retrieved June, 5, 2010. http://tez2.yok.gov.tr/

Kodotchigova, M. (2002). Role play in teaching culture: Six quick steps for classroom implementation. *The Internet TESL Journal, 8(7).* Retrieved June 5, 2010. *http://iteslj.org/Techniques/Kodotchigova-RolePlay.html*

Nunan, D. (2004). *Task-based language teaching.* Cambridge University Press.

Rantz, F. & Horan, P. (2005). Exploring Intercultural Awareness in the Primary Modern Language Classroom: The Potential of the New Model of European Language Portfolio Developed by the Irish Modern

Languages in Primary Schools Initiative (MLPSI). *Language and intercultural iommunication*, 5(3 & 4), 209 – 221.

Reichardt, C. S., & Cook, T. D. (1979). Beyond qualitative versus quantitative methods. In T. D. Cook & C. S. Reichardt (Eds.), *Qualitative and quantitative methods in evaluation research* (pp.7-32). Beverly Hills, CA: Sage.

Tomlinson, B. & Masuhara, H. (2004). Developing cultural awareness. *Modern English Teacher*, 13(1), 5-11.

Yıldırım, A., & Şimşek, H. (2008). *Sosyal bilimlerde nitel araştırma yöntemleri*. Ankara: Seçkin Yayıncılık.

Zalta, G. (2006). Using drama with children. *English teaching forum 44(2)*. Retrieved May 15, 2010. http://exchanges.state.gov/forum/vols/vol44/no2/p

In: Data Collection and Storage
Editor: Julian R. Eiras

ISBN 978-1-61209-689-6
© 2012 Nova Science Publishers, Inc.

Chapter 5

ANIMAL AND SEASONAL EFFECTORS OF COW BEHAVIOR IN DAIRY HOUSES: AN OBSERVATIONAL COLLECTION

A. Nikkhah[*] and R. Kowsar
[1]Department of Animal Sciences, University of Zanjan,
Zanjan 313-45195 Iran

ABSTRACT

Intuitively, in mechanized modern dairy facilities with competitive environments, monitoring behavior offers opportunities to manipulate and optimize nutritional, health and social status of high-merit cows. The objective was to collect and analyze seasonal data on various behaviors of lactating cows in different production and lactation stages during an observational study from December 2006 to February 2008. The large dairy herd had about 3000 dairy cattle housed in yards. A total of 415 multiparous high-producing cows (MH), 166 multiparous medium-producing cows (MM), 166 multiparous low-producing cows (ML), 165 primiparous high-producing cows (PH), 83 fresh cows (FC), 82 fresh heifers (FH), and 82 cows with high milk SCC (HSCC) were monitored. Seasonal eating, ruminating, standing and laying behaviors were recorded by 4 trained people at 1000 h weekly and on multiple days within weeks. Each activity was expressed as % of cows exhibiting the activity relative to the total number of cows in the yard. Feed was

---
[*] Correspondence: nikkhah@znu.ac.ir

delivered 6 times daily, 4 times as TMR at 0600, 1030, 1300, and 1800 h right after milking, and twice as top-dress alfalfa hay overnight. Across groups, greater percentages of cows were observed eating during winter (25.7%) than during spring (17.1%), summer (15.4%) and fall (14.5%). The percentage of cows neither eating nor ruminating was lower in winter (48.1%) than in summer (58.9%) and fall (58.6%), but not spring (53.7%). Greater proportions of cows in PH (24.6%) and ML (21.3%) groups were observed eating, compared to MM (15.2%), MH (16.6%) and FC (12.3%) groups. Lying was observed more often in FC (71%), MM (69.6%) and MH (64%) cows than in FH (54%), ML (55.7%) and PH (55.7%) cows. Greater proportions of cows were observed ruminating in MM (31.7%), FC (31.3%), HSCC (28.7%), PH (27.2%) and MH (26.7%) groups than in FH (20.5%) and ML (22.9%) groups. Uniquely, HSCC cows were relatively less active in eating and more active in laying. With the exceptionally and adequately large sample size and prolonged experimental period, data reveal determining effects of season alongside age, lactation stage, productivity and somewhat mastitis on eating, ruminating, and resting behaviors of lactating cows in large yards. The information fuel future designed study research and will be used to develop local and global guidelines for social and feeding begaviors to monitor cow health and welfare.

Keywords: Behavior, Eating, Ruminating, Season.

INTRODUCTION

In mechanized modern dairy facilities with competitive environments, monitoring behavior is an opportunity to manipulate and optimize nutritional, health and social status of high-merit cows. Initiative older research on cattle social behavior (Schmisseur et al., 1966; Arave and Albright, 1976; Arave et al., 1974; Lamb, 1976; Arave and Albright, 1981; Pennington and Albright, 1985), although very insufficient, highlighted and in some aspects quantified associations of cow physiology, social rank, immunity and performance with cow surroundings, including stalls design and space, inter-group member changes, isolation, and other stressors. The newer research shed light on how cow-grouping strategies affect social and feeding behaviors (Phillips and Rind, 2001; Albright, 1993; Grant and Albright. 2001). Most recently, renewed research interests on cow feed intake and social behavior have promised improvements in health, metabolism and production (Endres and

Barberg, 2007; Huzzey et al., 2007; von Keyserlingk et al., 2008; Goldhawk et al., 2009). For instance, Huzzey et al. (2007) showed that DMI and eating activity as well as engagement in social and aggressive interactions at feed bunk during the precalving week decrease in cows that are at high risk of mastitis postpartum. Similarly, Goldhawk et al. (2009) found that cows with 1) reduced DMI, 2) decreased frequency of feed bunk visits and 3) shorter feed bunk visits during the precalving week exhibited subclinical ketosis for few weeks around parturition. These studies suggest that social and feeding behaviors may affect and be affected by cow health and productivity. Thus, such behaviors can effectively be monitored as a management tool to evaluate and improve cow health and longevity, especially in large herds. Data are lacking on how environmental factors independently or in relation to cow factors (e.g., production level, parity, lactation stage) affect social-feeding behaviors. We hypothesized that lactating cows housed in large groups exhibit different eating, ruminating, and resting or social activities during different seasons. In addition, we hypothesized that such activities will depend on lactation stage, milk production level, and cow parity. Therefore, an observational study was conducted from December 2006 to February 2008 with the objective to collect and determine seasonal eating, ruminating, resting, standing and idle activities in lactating cows of different physiological stages.

MATERIALS AND METHODS

Cow Management and Behavior Monitoring

The herd had about 3000 dairy cattle including 1100 milking cows, housed in large yards based on stage of lactation and milk production. A total of 415 multiparous high-producing cows (MH), 166 multiparous medium-producing cows (MM), 166 multiparous low-producing cows (ML), 165 primiparous high-producing cows (PH), 83 fresh cows (FC), 82 fresh heifers (FH), and 82 cows with high milk SCC (HSCC) were monitored in different seasons. The average daily air temperature and relative humidity were respectively 20.9°C and 36% in spring, 26.8°C and 17.3% in summer, 10.0°C and 43.9% in fall, and 2.53°C and 55.8% in winter. During each season, eating, ruminating, standing and laying activities were recorded at 1000 h weekly and on multiple days within weeks by 4 individuals.

Table 1. Eating, ruminating, laying, idle and standing behaviors of dairy cows at different ages and production levels

Item	Cow group (CG)							Season				SEMc	SEMs	P-value	
	FC	FH	MH	MM	ML	PH	HSCC	Spring	Summer	Fall	Winter			CG	Season
Eating, %	12.6^c	20.4^{ab}	16.6^{bc}	15.2^{bc}	21.3^a	24.6^a	16.5^{bc}	17.1^b	15.4^b	14.5^b	25.7^a	2.0	2.7	<0.01	<0.01
Laying, %	71.0^a	54.0^c	64.0^a	69.6^a	55.7^c	55.7^c	65.3^{ab}	66.2	62.5	62.4	57.7	3.0	4.6	<0.01	0.32
Ruminating, %	31.3^{ab}	20.5^c	26.7^b	31.7^a	22.9^c	27.2^b	28.7^b	29.2	25.7	26.9	26.2	1.8	2.7	<0.01	0.72
Standing, %	15.6^{cd}	27.0^a	18.3^{bc}	13.8^d	21.7^b	17.2^c	19.0^{bc}	13.8	21.7	22.5	18.0	1.8	2.9	<0.01	0.12
Idle[1], %	56.1^a	59.1^a	56.7^a	53.1^b	55.8^{ab}	48.1^c	54.7^{ab}	53.7^{ab}	58.9^a	58.6^a	48.1^b	1.7	2.8	<0.01	<0.02

FC = fresh cows; FH = fresh, high-producing cows; MH = multiparous, high-producing cows; MM = multiparous, medium-producing cows; ML = multiparous, low-producing cows; PH = primiparous, high-producing cows; HSCC = high somatic cell counts cows.
^{a,b,c,d}Within each row under "cow group" and "season", means with different superscripts differ at P < 0.05.
[1] Percentage of cows neither eating nor ruminating.
SEMc = standard error of mean for cow group effect; SEMs = standard error of mean for season effect.

Table 2. Dietary feed ingredients and chemical composition of different concentrates (DM basis)

% of concentrate DM	Diet		
	Fresh	High-producing	Low-producing
Ground barley grain	35.0	43.0	33.0
Ground corn grain	10.3	4.5	0
Whole cottonseed	19.3	11.0	0
Cottonseed meal	4.2	3.5	3.5
Soybean meal	14.0	13.3	0
Wheat bran	0	4.0	30.0
Canola meal	4.2	11.0	11.0
Sunflower meal	0	0	16.4
Corn gluten	2.1	1.1	0
Fish meal	1.7	2.5	0
Limestone	1.4	1.1	1.4
Salt	0.2	0.5	0.5
Protected fat	2.1	1.1	0
Sodium bicarbonate	1.3	1.1	0
Magnesium oxide	0.2	0.2	0.2
Zeolite	0.7	0.9	2.0
Urea	0	0	0.7
Glycoline	1.4	0	0
Minerals and vit. Supplement[1]	1.8	1.2	1.3
Forage : concentrate	43 : 57	36 : 64	63 : 37
Alfalfa hay	24.4	19.6	29.1
Corn silage	18.8	16.6	19.4
Wheat straw	0	0	14.1
Chemical composition			
CP, %	19.2	20.8	16.8
NE_L[2], Mcal/kg	1.8	1.7	1.4

[1]Contained 196 g Ca, 96 g P, 71 g Na, 19 g Mg, 3 g Fe, 0.3 g Cu, 2 g Mn, 3 g Zn, 100 ppm Co, 100 ppm I, 0.1 ppm Se and 50 ×105 IU of vitamin A, 10 ×105 IU of vitamin D and 0.1 g of vitamin E/kg.
[2]NRC (2001).

At each recording, each activity was expressed as % of present cows exhibiting the activity relative to total number of cows in the yard. Cows were fed diets based on corn silage, alfalfa hay, barley and corn grains, cottonseeds, cottonseed and soybean meals, and wheat bran (Table 2). The average milk yield and milk fat % of the herd were 37 kg/d and 3.4%, respectively. The dietary forage to concentrate ratio was 36:64 for high-producing cows, 63:37 for low-producing cows, and 43:57 for fresh cows. Feed was delivered 6 times daily, 4 times as TMR at 0600, 1030, 1300 and 1800 h just after milking, and twice as top-dress overnight long alfalfa hay. The recording procedures and feeding and housing conditions were in accordance with the guidelines of the Iranian Council on Animal Care (1995).

Statistical Analysis

Data were analyzed as Mixed Models Procedures of SAS programs (SAS Institute, 2003). Final models consisted of fixed effects of cow group, season and the interaction, plus random effects of recording date within season, group within date, and residual errors. Least square means were estimated using REML method, and denominator degrees of freedom were calculated using Kenward-Roger method (SAS Institute, 2003). The PDIFF option of SAS program with Tukey test was used to separate means. Multiple means comparisons adjustment showed no significant interactions of season and cow group. The significance effects were declared at $P < 0.05$.

RESULTS AND DISCUSSION

Across groups, greater percentages of cows ($P < 0.01$) were observed eating during winter (25.7%) than during spring (17.1%), summer (15.4%), and fall (14.5%). This was consistent with the lower percentage of cows being idle in winter than in summer, suggesting greater needs for warming by spending more time eating in cold compared to warm seasons. Eating activity in cattle is known to entail expenditures equal to 10-30% of ME intake (Susenbeth et al., 1998). Winter time would be logical to require longer eating activities compared to warmer times. That would not necessarily mean reductions in nutrient use efficiency because increased heat production by increased eating can help to more effectively warm the cow body (NRC, 2001). The percentage of cows neither eating nor ruminating was less ($P < 0.05$) in winter (48.1%) than in summer (58.9%) and fall (58.6%) but not in spring (53.7%). This was consistent with the increased percentage of cows eating in winter than in other seasons.

More cows in PH (24.6%) and ML (21.3%) groups were observed eating compared with MM (15.2%), MH (16.6%), and FC (12.3%) groups. Fresh cows (FC) could be expectedly less active in eating compared to cows in more advanced stages of lactation, as DMI is rather low in fresh cows and yet to reach its peak (Grant and Albright, 2001; NRC, 2001). The result that HM and MM were observed less active in eating than LM cows suggests that with increased milk production, multiparous cows may eat faster to obtain certain amounts of nutrients. In addition, it can be suggested that higher producing multiparous cows with high social rank may spend more time ruminating after they rapidly consumed their required meals, compared to lower-producing multiparous cows (Grant and Albright, 2001). From a digestive physiology perspective, lower eating rate combined with longer eating time contribute to ensalivation (Beauchemin et al., 2008). Accordingly, forages cause much greater enslivation than concentrates (e.g., 3.4-7.2 vs. 1.1 g saliva/g DM; Beauchemin et al., 2008). This would justify why rumen acidosis severity and incidence increase shortly postpartum (Penner et al., 2007). As such, fresh and early lactation cows are expected to have reduced opportunities for ensalivation. However, high-producing primiparous cows could be an exception, since after parturition they do not experience as much dramatic changes in their physiology, immune function, and DMI as do multiparous cows (NRC, 2001). This characteristic is consistent with the active eating behavior in PH cows of the current study. Accordingly, laying was observed more often ($P < 0.01$) in FC (71%), MM (69.6%) and MH (64%) cows than in FH (54%), ML (55.7%) and PH (55.7%) groups.

More cows were observed ruminating ($P < 0.01$) in MM (31.7%), FC (31.3%), PH (27.2%) and MH (26.7%) groups compared to FH (20.5%) and ML (22.9%) groups. Rumination, by evolutionary definition, occurs when ruminants feel socially secure and are in fine psychological status, usually between morning and midday meals and after evening-grazing later overnight (Gordon and McAllister, 1970; Phillips, 2002). Fresh high-producing cows are characterized by most dramatic metabolic changes and challenges, suffering from inadequate DMI, lowered immunity and negative nutrient balance (NRC, 2001). Hence, in view of rumination psychophysiology, diurnal rumination patterns, and the fact that rumination in the present study was monitored in the morning, lower proportions of FH cows ruminating would be bio-meaningful. In addition, the resting saliva secretion is much lower (e.g., 50-100%) than the eating saliva secretion (Beauchemin et al.,

2008; Maekawa et al., 2002). Higher producing cows eat more DMI mainly because they eat longer and probably faster (Nikkhah et al., 2010), thus suggesting that reduced eating time in fresh cows may be related to reduced rumen acidosis tolerance (Penner et al., 2007).

The HSCC cows appeared to be relatively less active in eating compared to certain groups, such as PH and ML cows. Consistently, greater percentages of HSCC cows were observed laying compared to PH, ML, and FH groups. These novel results suggest some effect of subclinical mastitis on cow social and eating behaviors. In accordance with the most recent indications of using feeding and social behaviors as a prognosis for cows with upcoming risk for abnormalities such as metritis and subclinical ketosis (Goldhawk et al., 2009; Huzzey et al., 2007), our data highlight the simplicity and feasibility of monitoring cow behavior in large herds as a management tool for monitoring herd health. Given the exceptionally large sample size and prolonged experimental period, findings reveal novel determining effects of season alongside age, lactation stage and production on eating, ruminating, laying, standing and idle behaviors of dairy cows. Such extensive information fuel future designed study research and will be used to develop local and global guidelines for social and feeding behaviors to monitor cow health and welfare. Consequently, certain groups or individual cows with abnormal behavior can be taken under special control and care for prevention and optimum management strategies on health issues and production inconsistencies. Future behavior research with reasonable cow specificity within and between groups and varying degrees of mastitis is required.

CONCLUSION

Eating, ruminating, laying and standing behaviors of lactating cows housed in large yards within a 3000-head Holstein farm depended upon season, milk yield, lactation stage, parity and milk somatic cell counts. Monitoring behavior offers perspectives to optimize nutritional, health and social status of high-merit dairy cattle in mechanized settings with competitive environments. Varying behaviors reflect varying cow physiology, season-related environmental factors, feeding strategies and housing conditions. Thus, cow behavior requires to be seriously considered in the development of guidelines towards more sustainable dairy herds and industries.

ACKNOWLEDGMENTS

University of Zanjan and Isfahan University of Technology (Isfahan, Iran) are acknowledged for research and teaching facilities. The management board and employees of Ghyam Dairy Enterprise (Isfahan, Iran) are thanked for their diligent and continued cooperation. The Minstry of Science, Research and Technology, and University of Zanjan (Zanjan, Iran) are acknowledged for supporting Professor Dr. Akbar Nikkhah's programs in improving science education worldwide.

REFERENCES

Albright, J. L. (1993). Feeding behavior of dairy cattle. *J. Dairy Sci.* 76, 485-498.

Arave, C. W., & Albright, J. L. (1976). Social rank and physiological traits of dairy cows as influenced by changing group membership. *J. Dairy Sci.* 59, 974-981.

Arave, C. W. & Albright, J. L. (1981). Cattle behavior. *J. Dairy Sci.* 64, 1318-1329.

Arave, C. W., Albright, J. L. & Sinclair, C. L. (1974). Behavior, milk yield, and leucocytes of dairy cows in reduced space and isolation. *J. Dairy Sci.* 57, 1497-1501.

Beauchemin, K. A., Eriksen, L., Nørgaard, P. & Rode, L. M. (2008). Short Communication: Salivary secretion during meals in lactating dairy cattle. *J. Dairy Sci.* 91, 2077-2081.

Endres, M. I. & Barberg, A. E. (2007). Behavior of dairy cows in an alternative bedded-pack housing system. *J. Dairy Sci.* 90, 4192-4200.

Goldhawk, C., Chapinal, N., Veira, D. M., Weary, D. M. & von Keyserlingk, M. A. G. (2009). Prepartum feeding behavior is an early indicator of subclinical ketosis. *J. Dairy Sci.* 92, 4971-4977.

Gordon, J. G. & McAllister, I. K. (1970). The circadian rhythm of rumination. *J. Agric. Sci.* 85, 291-297.

Grant, R. J. & Albright, J. L. (2001). Effect of animal grouping on feeding behavior and intake of dairy cattle. *J. Dairy Sci.* 84, E156-163E.

Huzzey, J. M. Veira, D. M., Weary, D. M. & von Keyserlingk, M. A. G. (2007). Prepartum behavior and dry matter intake identify dairy cows at risk for metritis. *J. Dairy Sci.* 90, 3220-3233.

Iranian Council of Animal Care (1995). Guide to the Care and Use of Experimental Animals, Vol. 1. Isfahan University of Technology, Isfahan, Iran.

Lamb, R.C. (1976). Relationship between cow behavior patterns and management systems to reduce stress. *J. Dairy Sci.* 59, 1630-1636.

Maekawa, M., Beauchemin, K. A. & Christensen, D. A. (2002). Effect of concentrate level and feeding management on chewing activities, saliva production, and ruminal pH of lactating dairy cows. *J. Dairy Sci.* 85, 1165–1175.

Nikkhah, A., A. Soltani, H. Sadri, M. Alikhani, M. Babaei, A. Samie, G. R. Ghorbani. (2010). Optimizing Barley Grain Use by Dairy Cows: A Betterment of Current Perceptions. In Grain Production. Nova Science Publishers, Inc, NY, USA.

NRC. (2001). National Research Council. Nutrient requirements of dairy cattle. 7th rev. ed. National Acad. Sci. Washington, D.C.

Penner, G. B., Beauchemin, K. A. & Mutsvangwa, T (2007). Severity of ruminal acidosis in primiparous Holstein cows during the periparturient period. *J. Dairy Sci.* 90, 365–375.

Pennington, J. A. & Albright, J. L. (1985). Effect of feeding time, behavior, and environmental factors on the time of calving in dairy cattle. *J. Dairy Sci.* 68, 2746-2750.

Phillips, C. (2002). Cattle Behaviour and Welfare. Blackwell Science Ltd. Oxford, UK. pp 264.

Phillips, C. J. C. & Rind, M. I. (2001). The Effects on production and behavior of mixing uniparous and multiparous cows. *J. Dairy Sci.* 84, 2424-2429.

Schmisseur, W. E., Albright, J. L., Dillon, W. M., Kehrberg, E. W. & Morris, W. H. M. (1966). Animal behavior responses to loose and free stall housing. *J. Dairy Sci.* 49, 102-104.

Susenbeth, A., Mayer, R., Koehler, B. & Neumann, O. (1998). Energy requirement for eating in cattle. *J. Anim. Sci.* 76, 2701-2705.

Val-Laillet, D., Veira, D. M. & von Keyserlingk, M. A. G. (2008). Short communication: Dominance in free-stall—housed dairy cattle is dependent upon resource. *J. Dairy Sci.* 91, 3922-3926.

von Keyserlingk, M. A. G., Olenick, D. & Weary, D. M. (2008). Acute behavioral effects of regrouping dairy cows. *J. Dairy Sci.* 91, 1011-1016.

In: Data Collection and Storage
Editor: Julian R. Eiras

ISBN 978-1-61209-689-6
© 2012 Nova Science Publishers, Inc.

Chapter 6

SWIFT COLLECTION AND QUANTIFICATION OF COW CERVIX MORPHOLOGY DATA: VALIDATING A PRACTICAL APPARATUS

A. Nikkhah* and S. M. Karimzadeh

[1]Department of Animal Sciences, University of Zanjan, Zanjan 313-45195 Iran

ABSTRACT

Cow fertility has been affected adversely by increased milk production over the last few decades. Impaired uterine health and function postpartum followed by a failure to detect true estrus and breed cows timely are major contributors to depressed reproductive efficiency. The objective was to test and validate a designed monitoring system to videotape and quantify morphological characteristics of vagina and cervix in Holstein cows. The cervix and its surrounding area were videotaped during estrus and non-estrus days in two Holstein cows to score tissue morphology as altered by estrus. Cervix position, motility, secretions and distinctness were scored each on a 5-point scale basis, with score of 5 being central, very stable, highly mucosal, and distinct cervices, and score of 1 being entirely the other way. Results demonstrated that the cervix area was significantly ($P<0.01$) more discrete, more mucosal, more central, and more stable on the standing estrus days than on non-estrus days. During estrus, the cervix area was

---

* Correspondence: nikkhah@znu.ac.ir

clearly visible, and was rigidly positioned in the central terminal of vagina, whereas cervix in non-estrus days was unstable and hardly separable from its surroundings (shown in figures). Therefore, data validate the usefulness of the designed farm setting as an uncomplicated, inexpensive, and practical management tool in measuring and quantifying cow cervix morphological properties during different phases of the oestrus cycle. Future research on further quantification of reproductive tract physiology and health is required.

Keywords: cervix, apparatus, estrus, reproduction, dairy cow.

INTRODUCTION

The progressive advancements in the ruminant science and industry necessitate innovative, accurate and rapid technologies that can improve reproduction management. Simultaneous achievement of efficient production and reproduction has been a major challenge to dairy farmers (Moore and Thatcher, 2006; Studer, 1998). For instance, for many today's dairy farmers, a favorable calving interval is about 12-13 months (Norman et al., 2009; Strandberg and Oltenacu, 1989), which may not necessarily be optimum under given circumstances. To achieve such an interval, cows should not be under much stressful physiological and environmental conditions, such as heat and metabolic stresses (Jordan, 2003; Moore and Thatcher, 2006).

Improved fertility has been enabled by artificial insemination (AI) and monitoring physiological changes during the oestrus cycle (Senger, 1994). However, highly efficient AI requires highly skilled technical proficiency coupled with triumphant estrus detection, both of which are not easy to secure on modern farms (Redden et al., 1993; Senger, 1994). A common challenge to successful estrus detection is the occurrence of short and highly variable oestrus cycles that prevent managers from a timely monitoring of cow behavior and related cyclic reproductive events. For not detecting a single estrus expression, cow pregnancy is postponed by 21 days. Such a delayed conception elongates days-open and introduces irrecompenseable financial and time costs (Barr, 1975; Holmann et al., 1984).

Visual observation and tail painting (Xu et al., 1998), physical activity monitoring with pedometer (Løvendahl and Chagunda, 2010), perineal odors detection by electronic nose (Lane and Wathes, 1998), and milk progesterone levels (Moore and Spahr, 1991) have been used to capture estrus for a timely

AI conduct. However, these approaches are rather expensive, laborious, or overly technical (Williams et al., 1981). In addition, relying on only one method may rarely leads to a lasting success. Therefore, development of an uncomplicated, inexpensive, and accurate technique for complementary uses to the routine visual farm-staff observation is required. The objective was to test and validate a practical, on-farm apparatus for monitoring changes in cervical morphology. The morphology data were collected and compared quantitatively between standing estrus and non-estrus days.

MATERIALS AND METHODS

Animal Management and Experimental Conditions

This study was conducted at the Dairy Facilities of the University of Zanjan's Research Farm (Zanjan, Iran) during November of 2009. The Dairy Farm had a total of 190 Holstein cattle including 50 milking cows. Cows were milked 3 times daily at 0500, 1300, and 2100 h. Alfalfa hay and a barley grain based concentrate were delivered 3 and 4 times, respectively. Routinely, estrus heat was detected by assigned and trained farm staff, with cows being artificially inseminated 12 h after observing standing-estrus. The standing-estrus occurred when cow was prepared to be mounted by another cow. The herd had a voluntary waiting period of 50 days, calving to pregnancy interval of 134 days, calving to first breeding interval of 90 days, calving interval of 13.8 months, milking days of 305, first breeding conception rate of 50%, and overall conception rate of 56%. Pregnancy test was conducted by rectal palpation. For the purpose of the study, two black and white Holstein cows including one multiparous cow and one primiparous cow were selected. The cows were monitored all the time for reproductive events, namely estrus heat expression. During separate standing-estrus and non-estrus days, cervix area was videotaped using a practical, uncomplicated apparatus (Figure 1). The apparatus had a round shape with 45 cm length and 2.7 cm diameter with electrical settings inside and a polyvinyl cover outside. Lights were installed on the front side and electrical wires terminals were on the other end. The apparatus was connected to a laptp installed with a image capturing and processing software. Figure 1 shows the apparatus both separately and while inserted to the cow reproductive tract for cervical monitoring.

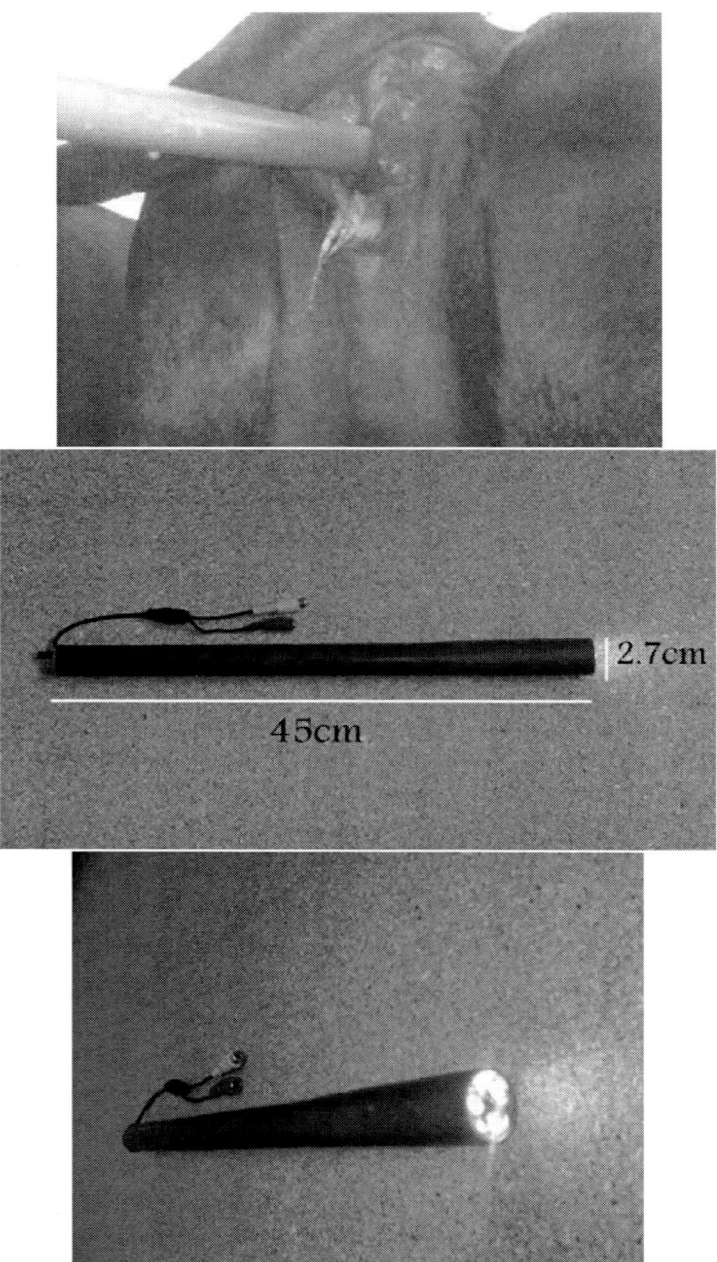

Figure 1. Schematics of the cervix-monitoring apparatus as inserted into the reproductive tract (top) and separately (middle and bottom)

Data Collection, Quantitative Assessment and Statistical Analysis

To quantify morphological properties of cervical regions, their a) distinctness, b) motility, c) central positioning, and d) mucosal secretions were scored each on a 5-point scale basis. The score of 5 represented a) highly separate and distinct view from the surrounding, b) static, c) fully central and stable, and d) highly mucosal cervices. The score of 1 characterized cervices in entirely the other way i.e., cervices were a) assorted with surrounding tissues, b) mobile, c) unstable, and d) non-mucosal or dry. The score of 2, 3, and 4 respectively represented mostly, moderately, and slightly a) distinct, b) static, c) central-stable, and d) mucosal cervices. The t-test was used to compare the scores between estrus and non-estrus days, ensuring homogeneity of variances (SAS Institute, 2003). In addition, mixed split-plot statistical models including fixed effect of recording day (estrus versus non-estrus) and random effects of cow within day plus residuals were developed. The P values < 0.05 were considered significant.

RESULTS AND DISCUSSION

As presented in Table 1 and shown in Figure 2, the cervix area was significantly ($P<0.01$) more split from its surrounding tissues, more mucosal, more central, and more stable on standing-estrus days than on non-estrus days. During standing-estrus days, cervices were clearly visible, and were rigidly positioned in the central end of vagina, whereas cervices in non-estrus days were unstable and were hardly separable from their surrounding regions (Figure 2). These quantitative, comparative, and reproducible data demonstrated and validated the on-farm feasibility and practicality of the monitoring apparatus in the definitive assessment of cervix morphology in dairy cattle during different phases of oestrus cycle. The recorded views, as shown in figures, show the reasonably consistent morphological and physiological properties of the cervical tissue within specific days of the reproductive cycle. This information promises potential in aiding more accurate estrus detection, particularly in cows with physiologically silent or hidden heat expression signs as well as in cows under special hormonal or managerial treatments.

Standing heat is when the cow is prepared to be mounted by another cow or a bull, which is a global standard sign for performing AI in about 12-15 h.

Such behavior is expressed following a surge in estrogen secretion and is associated with morphological changes in various tissues of the reproductive tract (Senger, 1994; Strandberg and Oltenacu, 1989). Thus, any reason or delay that results in not detecting estrus signs will change the shape of the lactation curve and can cause economical losses (De Vries, 2006; Norman et al., 2009). By decisively accurate estrus detections, with the aid of the monitoring apparatus developed in the current study, such productive and economical losses can be minimized. Moreover, a considerable number of repeat-breeder cows are those with repeated errors in estrus detection, for any possible reason (Barr, 1975; Senger, 1994). Furthermore, as frequently happens, even if well-trained, individuals in charge of visual observation are prone to prognostic errors, notably when more than one cow at a given time appear to be in estrus. In such instances, the present apparatus can prove especially more useful and complementary to minimizing doubts in diagnosing the right estrus cows at the right time. This will enable on-time breeding. In addition, due to its simple structure and methodology, any staff with minimal and brief training can proficiently practice the method. The very inexpensive apparatus (< 200 $US) can uniquely be utilized by also small-size dairy farmers. Future research on specific cows on other specific days of the oesterus cycle is required before maximum specificity and robustness in detailed quantification of the reproductive tract physiology and health can be guidelined.

Table 1. Quantitative assessment of cervical morphology parameters on standing-estrus and non-estrus days using a cervix-monitoring apparatus[1]

Parameter	Standing-estrus	Non-estrus	SEM	P-value
Cervix distinctness	4.5	2.3	0.3	< 0.01
Cervix motility	1.8	3.6	0.4	< 0.01
Cervix positioning	4.1	1.9	0.4	< 0.01
Cervix secretions	4.2	1.6	0.3	< 0.01

[1] Cervix a) distinctness, b) motility, c) central positioning, and d) mucosal secretions were scored each on a 5-point scale basis, with score of 5 being a) highly distinct from surrounding, b) fully central, c) fully stable and static, and d) highly mucosal cervices, and score of 1 being entirely the other way.

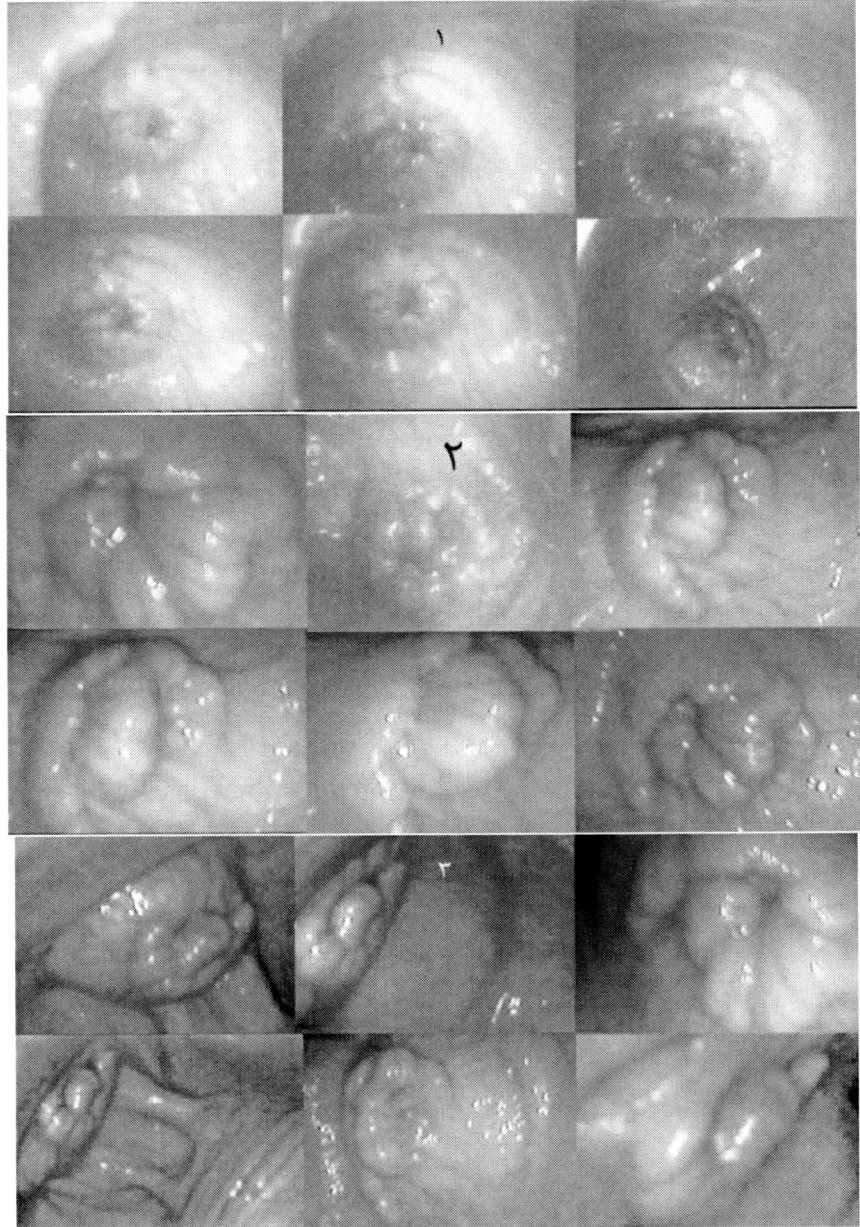

Figure 2. Cervical regions images on standing-estrus days (top) and non-estrus days (middle). The bottom images are various cervix positioning during non-estrus days.

Conclusion

An inexpensive and easy-to-handle on-farm apparatus was designed, manufactured, and tested to monitor, swiftly collect, and quantify cervix morphology information in dairy cows. Cervical regions were videotaped by the apparatus in two multiparous and primiparous black and white Holstein dairy cows during standing-estrus and non-estrus days of the oesterus cycle. Quantitative comparisons demonstrated that cervices were more distinct, more central, more mucosal, and highly stable on standing-estrus days than on non-estrus days. The visual data collected demonstrate and validate the on-farm feasibility and practicality of the apparatus for quantitative assessment of cervix morphology in dairy cattle. Findings suggest implications on the usefulness of the apparatus as a tool in monitoring ruminants' reproductive tract physiology and health.

Acknowledgments

The research and teaching facilities of the University of Zanjan (Zanjan, Iran) and diligent cooperation of the Research Dairy Farm's employees are thankfully acknowledged. The Minsitry of Science, Research and Technology (MSRT), and University of Zanjan (Zanja, Iran) are acknowledged for supporting A. Nikkhah's programs in improving science structuring and education in the new millennium worldwide.

References

Barr, H. L. (1975). Influence of estrus detection on days open in dairy herds. *J. Dairy Sci.* 58, 246-247.

De Vries, A. (2006). Economic value of pregnancy in dairy cattle. *J. Dairy Sci.* 89, 3876-3885.

Holmann F. J., Shumway C. R., Blake R. W., Schwart R. B. & Sudweeks E. M. (1984). Economic value of days open for Holstein cows of alternative milk yields with varying calving intervals. *J. Dairy Sci.* 67, 636-643.

Iranian Council of Animal Care. (1995). Guide to the Care and Use of Experimental Animals, vol. 1. Isfahan University of Technology, Isfahan, Iran.

Jordan, E. R. (2003). Effects of heat stress on reproduction. *J. Dairy Sci.* 86, E104-E114.

Lane, A. J. P. & Wathes, D. C. (1998). An electronic nose to detect changes in perineal odors associated with estrus in the cow. *J. Dairy Sci.* 81, 2145-2150.

Løvendahl, P. & Chagunda, M. G. G. (2010). On the use of physical activity monitoring for estrus detection in dairy cows. *J. Dairy Sci.* 93, 249-259.

Moore, A. S. & Spahr, S. L. (1991). Activity monitoring and an enzyme immunoassay for milk progesterone to aid in the detection of estrus. *J. Dairy Sci.* 74, 3857-3862.

Moore, K. & Thatcher, W. W. (2006). Major advances associated with reproduction in dairy cattle. *J. Dairy Sci.* 89, 1254-1266.

Norman, H. D., Wright, J. R., Hubbard, S. M., Miller, R. H. & Hutchison, J. L. (2009). Reproductive status of Holstein and Jersey cows in the United States. *J. Dairy Sci.* 92, 3517-3528.

Redden, K. D., Kennedy, A. D., Ingalls, J. R. & Gilson, T. L. (1993). Detection of estrus by radiotelemetric monitoring of vaginal and ear skin temperature and pedometer measurements of activity. *J. Dairy Sci.* 76, 713-721.

SAS User's Guide. (2003). Version 9.1. Edition. SAS Institute Inc., Cary, NC.

Senger, P. L. (1994). The estrus detection problem: new concepts, technologies, and possibilities. *J. Dairy Sci.* 77, 2745-2753.

Studer, E. (1998). A veterinary perspective of on-farm evaluation of nutrition and reproduction. *J. Dairy Sci.* 81, 872-876.

Strandberg E. & Oltenacu P.A. (1989). Economic consequences of different calving intervals. *Acta Agric. Scan.* 39, 407-420.

Williams, W. F., Yver, D. R. & Gross, T. S. (1981) Comparison of estrus detection techniques in dairy heifers. *J. Dairy Sci.* 64, 1738-1741.

Xu, Z. Z., McKnight, D. J., Vishwanath, R., Pitt, C. J. & Burton, L. J. (1998). Estrus detection using radiotelemetry or visual observation and tail painting for dairy cows on pasture. *J. Dairy Sci.* 81, 2890–2896.

INDEX

A

access, 9, 18
acidosis, 91, 92, 94
adjustment, 40, 90
adults, 25
advancement, 76
advancements, ix, 96
age, vii, viii, 6, 12, 15, 17, 27, 28, 54, 72, 79, 81, 86, 92
air temperature, 87
Alaska, 19
Alaska Natives, 19
alfalfa, 86, 90
algorithm, 10, 12, 20, 23, 46
amplitude, 28, 29, 38, 39, 42, 55
anxiety, 78
assessment, 9, 25, 99, 100, 102
atmosphere, 78, 80
awareness, 2, 73, 74, 79, 80, 82, 83

B

bandwidth, 33
banks, vii, 28
base, viii, 4, 10, 54, 80
beams, 30, 31, 32, 33, 43, 44
behaviors, ix, 85, 86, 88, 92
Belgium, 4, 5, 6, 14
bias, 54, 57, 72, 74, 75, 79
bicarbonate, 89
biodegradable materials, 32
birefringence, 39, 40
Boltzmann constant, 60, 66
breast cancer, 11, 12, 16, 20, 22, 23, 24, 25
breeding, 97, 100
budget allocation, 2, 9
building blocks, 58
burn, 79

C

calibration, 39
cancer, vii, 2, 3, 7, 8, 9, 10, 11, 12, 13, 14, 15, 16, 17, 18, 19, 20, 22, 23, 24
carcinoma, 23
case study, 80
cattle, viii, 85, 86, 87, 90, 92, 93, 94, 97, 99, 102, 103
Census, 12
cerebrovascular disease, 23
certification, 8
cervix, vii, 95, 96, 97, 98, 99, 100, 101, 102
challenges, 18, 91
charge coupled device, 44
chemical, 62, 89
chemotherapy, 10, 24
children, 79, 80, 83

circadian rhythm, 93
classes, 12, 72
classification, 5, 19
classroom, 79, 82
clusters, 68
coding, 5, 6, 9, 10, 12, 14, 15, 21, 22, 23
coherence, 2, 7, 9, 55, 73
colorectal cancer, 23, 24
commercial, 74
communication, 67, 71, 73, 74, 78, 80, 94
communication strategies, 73
complexity, 38, 55
complications, 21, 22, 24
composites, 56
composition, 32, 66, 89
computation, 54
computer, 44
computing, 54, 68
conception, 96, 97
condensation, 60, 61
configuration, 42, 48
construction, 77
consumers, 6
cooling, 62
cooperation, 93, 102
copper, 56, 57
cost, 4, 6, 32, 54
critical thinking, 74
cross-validation, 15
crystalline, 54, 56, 63
crystals, 50, 56, 63
cultural differences, 79
culture, 71, 73, 74, 77, 79, 80, 81, 82
cycles, 66, 96
cytology, 7
Czech Republic, 8

D

danger, 76
data collection, vii, 3, 8, 10, 19, 78, 80
data processing, 68
data set, 4
database, 6, 10, 12, 13, 14, 15, 16, 17, 20, 24

deaths, 6
defects, 49
Denmark, 5, 6, 13, 24
dependent variable, 80
deposition, 54, 57, 63, 64, 66
depression, 25
destiny, 60
detection, 10, 96, 99, 100, 102, 103
detection techniques, 103
developed countries, 7
deviant behaviour, 73
diabetes, 25
diaphragm, 30, 43, 44
diffraction, 30, 33, 34, 35, 36, 37, 38, 43, 46, 48, 65
discordance, 11, 15, 16
diseases, 10
distinctness, 95, 99, 100
distribution, 45
diversity, 74
drawing, 13
dry matter, 93
dysplasia, 20

E

economic status, 9, 18, 19
economics, vii, 3
editors, 19, 22
education, viii, 72, 81, 82, 93, 102
educational research, 75
elderly population, 12
electric field, viii, 54, 57, 66, 68
electrical properties, 65, 66
electron, 64
emergency, 7
emotional responses, 74
empathy, 74, 79, 80
employees, 93, 102
emulsions, 32
encryption, 18
energy, 29, 32, 34, 36, 41, 55, 61, 62, 63, 65, 68, 79
energy density, 62, 65
English Language, 71

entropy, 59, 60, 61
environment, 76, 80
environmental conditions, ix, 96
environmental factors, ix, 87, 92, 94
enzyme, 103
enzyme immunoassay, 103
epidemiology, vii, 2, 3, 8, 18, 20
equilibrium, 60, 61, 62, 67
estrogen, 100
ethnocentrism, 74
Europe, 7
evidence, 73
evolution, 3, 54
examinations, 65
excitation, 56
expenditures, 90
exploitation, 43
exposure, 30, 32, 35, 36, 37, 46, 47, 48, 80

F

fabrication, 29
false negative, 11, 15
false positive, 11, 15
farmers, ix, 96, 100
farms, 96
fat, 89, 90
fears, 18
fertility, 95, 96
films, 54, 57, 58, 63, 64, 65, 66, 68
financial, 3, 6, 9, 10, 12, 17, 18, 96
Finland, 13, 21
fixation, 62
foreign language, 81, 82
formation, 67
formula, 14
France, 1, 4, 5, 7, 13, 15, 20, 23
freedom, 90
funding, 6, 19
funds, 19

G

galaxies, 67
Gaussian equation, 45

general practitioner, 10, 12
geography, 22
geometry, 33, 57
Germany, 5, 53
globalization, 19
grades, 72
gratings, 29, 30, 34, 37, 38, 48
grazing, 91
group membership, 93
grouping, ix, 86, 93
growth, 6, 66
guidance, 78
guidelines, 86, 90, 92

H

health, vii, viii, 1, 2, 3, 4, 7, 8, 9, 11, 12, 13, 18, 19, 22, 24, 85, 86, 92, 95, 100, 102
health care, vii, 3, 4, 11, 19
health care system, 3
health information, vii, 3, 22
health insurance, 4, 7, 13
health services, 18, 24
health status, 19
height, 66
histology, 19
hologram, 30, 31, 32, 33, 34, 35, 36, 37, 44, 45, 46
homogeneity, 28, 29, 38, 99
hospice, 25
hospitalization, 4
housing, 90, 92, 93, 94
human, viii, 25, 54, 76
human condition, 25
humidity, 87
Hungary, 5, 7
hybrid, 28, 29, 38, 42, 48
hypothesis, 59

I

ideal, viii, 72
identification, 10, 13, 14, 16, 23
identity, 14

image, 40, 44, 45, 46, 48, 49, 57, 97
images, 44, 45, 46, 48, 64, 101
immune function, 91
immunity, viii, 86, 91
improvements, ix, 17, 86
incidence, vii, 2, 3, 7, 8, 9, 10, 11, 12, 13, 15, 16, 17, 18, 19, 20, 23, 24, 25, 31, 91
independent variable, 80
Indians, 19
individuals, 17, 18, 74, 76, 87, 100
industries, 92
industry, ix, 96
information processing, vii, 27, 28, 54, 55
information technology, 55
ingredients, 89
interference, 30, 32, 44
International Classification of Diseases, 21
Iran, 85, 93, 94, 95, 97, 102
Ireland, 8, 13
isolation, viii, 86, 93
issues, 12, 92
Italy, 5, 6
iteration, 35, 36, 37

J

Japan, 5
Jordan, ix, 96, 103
justification, 76

L

lactation, ix, 85, 87, 91, 92, 100
language acquisition, viii, 72
languages, 82
laws, 18, 59
lead, 57
leakage, 55
learners, 72, 73, 74, 77, 78, 79, 80, 82
learning, 71, 73, 74, 75, 79, 81, 82
legislation, 18
lens, 30, 43, 44
light, ix, 28, 29, 30, 31, 32, 38, 39, 44, 65, 81, 86

light beam, 38
linguistics, 82
longevity, ix, 87
lung cancer, 23
Luo, 51

M

magnitude, 28, 29, 40, 55
management, vii, ix, 3, 4, 6, 87, 92, 93, 94, 96
manipulation, 68
Maryland, 4
mass, 57, 59
mastitis, ix, 86, 87, 92
material surface, 33, 44
materials, 29, 32, 55, 56, 68
matter, iv, 81
measurement, 76
measurements, 66, 103
media, 31, 54, 59, 61
Medicaid, 7, 12, 13, 23
medical, 8, 9, 10, 11, 12, 15, 17, 20, 22
Medicare, 4, 6, 12, 13, 16, 20, 21, 23, 24, 25
melanoma, 12
memory, vii, viii, 27, 28, 29, 33, 37, 48, 53, 54, 55, 58, 65, 77
metabolic changes, 91
metabolism, ix, 86
metals, viii, 54
methodology, 28, 29, 75, 100
microscope, 30, 31, 43, 44
migration, 11, 17
mixing, 94
models, 2, 15, 17, 90, 99
modules, 82
molecules, 39
morbidity, 2, 3, 8, 21, 22
morphology, vii, 95, 97, 99, 100, 102
mortality, vii, 2, 7, 8, 18, 19, 20
mortality rate, 8
Moscow, 53
motivation, 72, 74, 75
music, vii, 27, 28, 82

Index

N

nanostructures, viii, 54
nanotechnology, viii, 54
nanotube, viii, 54, 55
national identity, 13, 18
National Research Council, 94
negative attitudes, 81
neglect, 75
Netherlands, 8, 13
Norway, 5
nuclei, 65
nursing, 4
nursing home, 4
nutrient, 90, 91
nutrients, 91
nutrition, 103

O

one dimension, 31, 74
opportunities, 85, 91
optical anisotropy, 39
optical properties, 32
optimization, 32, 39, 40, 41, 42
overlap, 30, 31, 33

P

palpation, 97
parallel, 31, 33, 35
parallelism, 55
parity, ix, 87, 92
participants, 73
pasture, 103
pathology, 7, 10
patient care, 8
perinatal, 22, 25
permittivity, 55, 57
phase boundaries, 60
Philadelphia, 82
photons, 60
physical activity, 96, 103
physicians, 4, 8
physiology, viii, 86, 91, 92, 96, 100, 102
plane waves, 30
play activity, 80
polarity, 66, 67
polarization, 38, 39
policy, 12, 19
population, vii, 2, 3, 7, 8, 9, 11, 12, 13, 14, 15, 16, 17, 18, 23
Portugal, 4, 5, 6, 7
positive attitudes, 81
preeclampsia, 22
pregnancy, 22, 96, 97, 102
preparation, iv, 58, 65, 66
prevention, 92
primary school, 77
principles, 20
probability, 45, 55
probability distribution, 45
professionals, vii, 3, 4, 18
progesterone, 96, 103
prognosis, 2, 8, 92
project, 14, 75
prostate cancer, 12, 23, 24, 25
protection, 18
prototype, viii, 28
psychiatry, 7
public health, vii, 3, 9, 25
pulmonary embolism, 23
P-value, 88, 100

Q

qualitative research, 78
quality assurance, 9
quality control, 9
quantification, vii, 96, 100
quantitative research, 76, 77
quantum bits, 54
quantum computing, viii, 54
quantum state, 54
qubits, 54, 55
questionnaire, 77, 78, 79

R

race, 12
radiation, 24, 53, 59, 60, 61, 62, 67
radiation therapy, 24
radiotherapy, 10
reading, 34, 65, 80
real numbers, 55
real time, 28, 29, 38
recommendations, iv, 7
reconstruction, 30, 33, 38, 44, 45
red shift, 67
reference system, 40
reform, viii, 72
refractive index, 32, 39
registries, 2, 7, 9, 11, 13, 14, 15, 16, 17, 18, 20, 22, 23
Registry, 24
regression, 15, 16
regression analysis, 16
regression model, 16
rehabilitation, 7
reliability, 55
relief, 64
reproduction, ix, 96, 103
reputation, 11
requirements, 18, 94
researchers, vii, 4, 8, 18, 27, 28, 72, 75, 76
residual error, 90
residuals, 99
resistance, 58, 66, 67
resolution, 32, 49
resources, 75
response, 32
restrictions, 18
retardation, 38
risk, ix, 18, 23, 87, 92, 93
room temperature, viii, 53, 54, 57, 58, 65
roots, 34
rotation axes, 33
rotation axis, 31
rules, 6, 73
rural areas, 12
Russia, 68

S

saliva, 91, 94
saturation, 57
science, vii, ix, 27, 28, 93, 96, 102
second language, viii, 72, 82
secretion, 91, 93, 100
security, 14, 25
selectivity, 29, 33, 34
semiconductor, vii, 53, 55, 63, 66, 68
semiconductors, 54
semi-structured interviews, 79
sensitivity, 11, 12, 14, 15, 16, 18, 20, 25, 29, 32, 34
sex, 15
shape, 97, 100
signs, 99, 100
silicon, 53, 56, 67
silver, 32, 56, 57
Singapore, 5, 6, 7
single crystals, 63
skin, 12, 103
skin cancer, 12
social activities, ix, 87
social behavior, viii, 86, 92
social phenomena, 76
social rules, 73
social security, 13, 14
social status, viii, 73, 85, 86, 92
sociology, vii, 3
software, 14, 97
solar cells, 56
solution, 61
somatic cell, 88, 92
Spain, 27
specialists, 8
spending, 90
spin, 54
spontaneity, 79
Spring, 88
stability, 16, 32, 56, 61, 66
standard deviation, 45
standard error, 88
state, 20, 39, 40, 42, 55, 60, 62, 68, 77, 83
states, 18, 39, 40, 42, 54, 55, 58

statistics, 7
stoichiometry, 63
storage, vii, viii, 27, 28, 29, 32, 34, 37, 38, 39, 40, 41, 46, 47, 48, 49, 51, 54, 55, 56, 63, 65, 67, 68
storage media, 56, 67
stress, 94, 103
stressors, viii, 86
stroke, 21
structure, 54, 57, 58, 59, 64, 68, 100
structuring, 102
style, 76
substrate, 63, 64, 66, 67
substrates, 53, 63, 65, 66
Sun, 68, 69
superconductivity, viii, 54
supervisor, 76
survival, 25
Sweden, 5, 6, 7, 8
Switzerland, 5

T

target, 63, 71, 74, 75, 77, 79, 81
teachers, 71, 73, 75, 77, 81
teaching experience, 81
technical efficiency, 18
techniques, vii, 14, 18, 25, 27, 28, 29, 79
technologies, vii, ix, 27, 28, 63, 96
technology, 51, 55, 64
temperature, viii, 54, 56, 60, 62, 63, 64, 65, 66, 67, 68, 103
terminals, 97
testing, 82
therapy, 16
thermodynamic equilibrium, 61, 62
thermodynamics, 59
thin films, vii, 54, 63, 68
thinning, 55
third dimension, 55
thrombosis, 23
thyroid, 15, 17, 20, 22, 23
thyroid cancer, 15, 17, 20, 22, 23
time periods, 16
time use, 35

tissue, 95, 99
training, 76, 100
traits, 93
transformation, 61
transmission, 40
transparency, 6, 57
transport, 66
treatment, 18, 23, 24, 25
triangulation, 76
tumor, 24
tumours, 7, 10
tunneling, 54, 55, 57, 66
Turkey, viii, 71, 72, 75, 76, 81
twist, 39

U

Ukraine, 53
uniform, 6, 34, 35, 36, 43, 45
United, 4, 5, 13, 50, 103
United Kingdom (UK), 4, 5, 6, 7, 12, 13, 50, 94
United States (USA), 4, 5, 6, 7, 13, 82, 94, 103
unstructured interviews, 78
urban, 17

V

vacuum, 63
vagina, 95, 99
validation, 9, 13, 17, 21, 22, 23
variables, 6, 13, 14, 73, 79
variations, 7, 9, 11, 12, 18, 61, 62
vector, 55
vein, 23
velocity, 56, 57
videotape, 95
vitamin A, 89
vitamin D, 89
vitamin E, 89
vocabulary, 71, 73, 74, 82

W

Washington, 22, 94
water, 81
wavelengths, 32
web, 82
welfare, 86, 92
windows, 72, 75
wires, 67, 97
worldwide, 2, 8, 19, 93, 102

writing process, 56

X

X-ray diffraction, 54

Y

Yale University, 4
yield, 8, 55, 90, 92, 93